The Writer's Hustle

The Writer's Hustle

A Professional Guide to the Creativity, Discipline, Humility, and Grit Every Writer Needs to Flourish

JOEY FRANKLIN

BLOOMSBURY ACADEMIC
LONDON • NEW YORK • OXFORD • NEW DELHI • SYDNEY

BLOOMSBURY ACADEMIC
Bloomsbury Publishing Plc
50 Bedford Square, London, WC1B 3DP, UK
1385 Broadway, New York, NY 10018, USA
29 Earlsfort Terrace, Dublin 2, Ireland

BLOOMSBURY, BLOOMSBURY ACADEMIC and the Diana logo are
trademarks of Bloomsbury Publishing Plc

First published in Great Britain 2023
Reprinted 2023

Copyright © Joey Franklin, 2023
Illustrations © Kath Richards, 2023

Joey Franklin has asserted his right under the Copyright, Designs and
Patents Act, 1988, to be identified as Author of this work.

For legal purposes, the Acknowledgments on p. x constitute an extension of
this copyright page.

Cover design: Kath Richards
Cover image © Kath Richards

A catalogue record for this book is available from the British Library.

A catalog record for this book is available from the Library of Congress.

ISBN: HB: 978-1-3501-6074-3
PB: 978-1-3501-6075-0
ePDF: 978-1-3501-6076-7
eBook: 978-1-3501-6077-4

Typeset by Deanta Global Publishing Services, Chennai, India
Printed and bound in Great Britain

To find out more about our authors and books visit www.bloomsbury.com and
sign up for our newsletters.

*To My Father-in-Law, Michael, who is typing away
on clouds of glory*

"A writer who waits for ideal conditions under which to work will die without putting a word on paper."—E. B. White

CONTENTS

ACKNOWLEDGMENTS

I am grateful to all the curious, brilliant, disciplined, creative, and generous writers who offered up the stories and advice that make up so much of this book. And I'm likewise grateful to all the students I've taught over the years—for writing with such astounding vulnerability and passion, and for asking so many of the questions that this book hopes to answer. I am also deeply indebted to my many writing mentors—first and foremost to Patrick Madden whose constant encouragement has been essential these many years, but also to Jill Patterson, Dennis Covington, Dinty W. Moore, Diana Hume George, Kyle Minor, and the Late Doug Thayer. Each in their own way has helped shape who I am today.

Many thanks as well to the editors and reviewers who helped me develop this project: Sean Prentiss for encouraging me to pitch the book to Bloomsbury, and to Lucy Brown for her guidance at every step along the way. And thanks as well to the colleagues and mentors who read early drafts of various chapters: Lance Larsen, Spencer Hyde, Nicole Walker, Stephen Tuttle, Phong Nguyen, and Jamin Rowan. Also thanks to my research assistants: Becca Evans, Shelby Johnson, and especially Kath Richards for her excellent illustration and design work, and to the English Department and College of Humanities at Brigham Young University for funding their efforts.

Finally, a special thanks to my wife, Melissa, not only for lending her love and support, but also her expertise in design and pedagogy as we've discussed the details of this project over the past three years. And to our three sons, for not thinking their father too lame as he types away at the keyboard. Each word has always been for them.

And by way of acknowledgement, portions of Chapter 7, "Submitting Work," and Chapter 8, "Considering (More) School" come originally (and in slightly different form) from two of my earlier publications: "Submit That Manuscript: Why Submission should be the final step in your Writing Process." *Poets & Writers* 45.4 (2017) 65–69, and "The Fine Art of Selecting a Program: Five Reasons to Consider an MA." *Poets & Writers* 26.6 (2015): 109–115.

ABOUT THE AUTHOR AND ILLUSTRATOR

Author

Joey Franklin has taught creative writing and literature in Ohio, Texas, and Utah, and he is the author of two essay collections, *Delusions of Grandeur: American Essays* (2020), and *My Wife Wants You to Know I'm Happily Married* (2015). His essays have appeared in such magazines as *Gettysburg Review*, *Hunger Mountain*, *Ninth Letter*, and *Brevity*, and he has published articles on craft, theory, and professionalization in *The Writer's Chronicle*, *Poets & Writers Magazine*, *Assay*, and *Triquarterly*. He is an associate professor of English at Brigham Young University where he has served as coordinator for the MFA program and helped develop a creative writing minor. Since 2019, he has coedited the literary journal *Fourth Genre: Explorations in Nonfiction*, and he lives in Provo, Utah, with his wife, Melissa, their three sons, and a dog named Virginia Woof.

Illustrator

Kath Richards holds an MFA in creative writing and a bachelor's of science in technology engineering, both from Brigham Young University. While an MFA student, she served as editor-in-chief of the literary magazine *Inscape,* helped coordinate the BYU English Department Reading Series, and helped organize YANCON, a local conference for writers of young adult fiction. She is the managing editor of *Soft Union*, a literary biweekly.

FIGURES

INTRODUCTION: THE WRITER'S HUSTLE

This is a book about hustle. And I don't throw that word around lightly. Especially since it took so much convincing for Bloomsbury to let me use it in the first place. The word does, after all, come with plenty of baggage. In Hollywood, hustle is the purview of pool sharks, poker players, and pimps. In business, where it's meant to conjure the entrepreneurial spirit, hustle often conjures instead the spirit of used car lots and timeshare seminars. One poet that I hoped to interview for this book expressed grave concerns about the word, telling me emphatically that "the hustle(r) mentality" had no place in the life of a creative writer.

But there's also the hustle of athletes. Players who set the tone for their teammates, who work harder, who stay longer at practice, and who give that extra kick in the last few minutes of a game. It's the kind of hustle celebrated on posters at the gym ("Good things happen to those who hustle" and "The dream is free. Hustle sold separately," for instance). But that's not exactly the hustle I'm driving at here either.

Instead, consider all the work that writers do when they're not actually placing words on the page. Certainly an hour or an afternoon or a year at the keyboard takes hustle (think of Hemingway rewriting the last page of *Farewell to Arms* thirty-nine times all in the name of "getting the words right"[1]), but the writer's hustle is about much more than hours at the keyboard. It's the work writers do in preparation for that keyboard time. And it's the work they do afterward too.

It's the hustle of Joan Didion and her lifelong habit of writing in a journal to "keep on nodding terms" with her former selves.[2] And it's the hustle of Cheryl Strayed whose commitment to her Portland writing group helped her finish her best-selling memoir, *Wild*.[3] But it's also the hustle of Emily Dickinson who wrote hundreds of poems all on her own and then sought out a mentor because, as she put it, "the mind is so near itself it cannot see distinctly."[4] It's the hustle of Man Booker Prize–winner Marlon James, who pushed through nearly eighty rejections before publishing his first novel.[5] And it's the hustle of Colson Whitehead, who, with his eight-page-per-week goal has (as of the time of this writing) produced ten books, including two Pulitzer Prize winners.[6]

Of course, it's also the hustle of thousands of writers working outside the spotlight. The eighteen-year-old filling his first notebook with poetry. The graduate student up late reading another novel. The accountant who's finally going on that writing retreat to polish up her memoir. The citizen journalist recording podcasts in his closet; social media book reviewers spreading the good word of good writing online; a legion of volunteers organizing readings, open-mic nights and literary festivals; a global community of online creators supporting and encouraging one another, and thousands of other writers putting in the work each day, sometimes producing what they love, sometimes what pays the bills, each of them in their own way making room for writing in their lives.

This is the hustle of being a writer. It's about a desire to participate in the larger conversation, to celebrate what's out there, and to contribute something of our own. It's about creative problem solving on and off the page and about being confident enough to believe in our work while staying humble enough to ask for help. It's about cultivating the discipline to treat writing like work and the patience necessary to forgive ourselves when we fall short of our own expectations.

To be clear, I'm not interested in a single *right way* to navigate the writing life. Instead, I'm interested in the countless ways writers have found to accomplish their own goals. The path to writerly success is personal, idiosyncratic, and always subject to change, delay, and detour. It's not about walking a single predetermined route but about observing how others have made their own way and then, with those models as guides, setting out to establish our own right path.

With that in mind, I've organized this book so that we can follow more or less the arc of a writer's development. We begin with a granular look at living the day-to-day life of a writer. Then we discuss the role of writing groups and formal workshops and the value of mentors and participating in the writing community. We then move on to consider the purpose of writing conferences, residencies, and retreats, followed by some detailed strategies for finishing writing projects and a crash course on the many ways to get those projects out into the world. Then, in the home stretch, we take a look at the potential benefits of a formal creative writing education and discuss professional opportunities for creative writers in and out of the academy. Finally, we end our long discussion on the writer's hustle by considering ways of maintaining that hustle over a lifetime.

Each chapter includes anecdotes and advice drawn from dozens of personal interviews with a diverse group of writers as well as information gleaned from an intensive scouring of writing manuals, guidebooks, published interviews, magazine articles, blog posts, advice forums, YouTube videos, and podcasts. I've also included a few notes from my own life as a writer. Of course, no book can contain all the information a writer needs, so it's best to think of each chapter as a primer. Then, for more information as well as for sample documents, case studies, extended interviews, resource links and other material, you can visit the book's companion website, joeyfranklin.com/writershustle.

This project was born of all the questions my students ask me about the writing life, and I originally envisioned it as a companion text for an entire creative writing education, a resource to accompany a writer from the first undergraduate workshop all the way through graduate school and beyond. But everything here applies to all writers, be they freelancers, starving artists, new-media hopefuls, or tentative hobbyists. After all, it's not a diploma that turns any of us into writers. And it's not publication either. It's not who we know, where we work, or how many people follow us on social media. The only metric that matters on any given day is whether or not we've put in the work. And the only virtue that will sustain that work is hustle—that peculiar combination of creativity, discipline, humility, and grit that every writer needs to flourish.

I hope this book helps you cultivate more of your own.

1.

MAKING THE MOST OF EACH DAY

We begin our discussion with the dictum "Write what you know," which is an old one, but not entirely helpful. To say that writing can come only from lived experience is a little like saying we can make a recipe only for food we've already tasted. It demands we turn our backs on imagination, empathy, research, and experimentation. Indeed, the famous challenge from Henry James to "be one of the people upon whom nothing is lost"[1] was a direct response to this tired injunction. *Sure,* he seems to argue, *write from your own experience, but make your experience as broad and deep and rich as possible.* To James, experience was about examining the inner workings of the mind and cultivating "the power to guess the unseen from the seen, to trace the implication of things, to judge the whole piece by the pattern."

To experience the world as a writer is to pay attention, which, in the twenty-first century, is no easy task. Our creative lives must compete with day jobs; with homework; with lovers, children, and pets; with leaky faucets and empty coffee pots; with Twitter, Reddit, and Netflix. And yet, perhaps thinking in terms of competition is shortsighted. We may be living in an age of distraction, but what if the distractions of the world could be transformed into sources of inspiration? What if the day-to-day life of a writer is less about building walls around ourselves to keep the chaos out and more about adopting habits to help keep our creative impulses alive despite all the chaos? Certainly, we all need a bit of solitude to get our writing done, but there's a lot that we can do between writing sessions to make the most of life as it unfolds.

Habit #1: Observe

Which is to say, do more than simply see. Think of how we use that word—*observe*. Poll watchers on Election Day, psychologists in the laboratory, tourists at the top of a building to "take it all in." Observation implies a will to understand, to make connections, to see the big picture.

For most writers, observation is an essential first step in the creative process. Take Ursula K. Le Guin, who writes, "I got whatever knowledge I have of the hearts and minds of human beings, through imagination working on observation."[2] But to marry observation and imagination, we must not merely "write what we know;" as novelist Lee Child puts it, we must "write what you feel."[3] Writing well means cultivating a passion for humanity marked by all the emotion of a passionate relationship: joy, anticipation, and ecstasy but also fear, anxiety, and pain. "Everyone thinks writers must know more about the inside of the human head," writes Margaret Atwood. "But that's wrong. They know less, that's why they write. Trying to find out what everyone else takes for granted."[4] I hope you hear in that an echo of Henry James—we can only be the kind of person on whom nothing is lost when we refuse to take anything for granted.

In practical terms, observation means keeping ourselves open to our inner and outer experience. "Everything you read, see, hear, or experience is a potential subject," writes novelist Jewell Parker Rhodes. "Every idea, intuition, or ancestral tie you investigate helps you become a better, more thoughtful writer."[5] Novelist Tim Denevi keeps himself "constantly on the lookout for moments when [he is] genuinely surprised; not just by some incident, but by a fact, or even a physical space. Moments when [he finds himself] inhabited by an idea, an interaction between two people, or by an event in history."[6]

Observation means relishing the complexity of the natural and social world, it means charting the winds and whims of history, and it means, ultimately, becoming a seismograph for the trembling human heart. It means paying attention to the humanity in our daily interactions, and it means seeking out experiences too. Young adult (YA) novelist Jodi Picoult, for example, has dined with a Yup'ik tribe, lived on an Amish dairy farm, visited with death-row inmates, and even "lain down on the table where they're given lethal injections."[7]

But observation doesn't always require a field trip. YA novelist Martine Leavitt explains, "the first skill of the writer is to learn how to live imaginatively in the body of another being." Leavitt works in fiction, but her approach applies to all literary art. Creating characters, imagining readers, giving voice to poetic personas, or portraying the people in our own lives all require that we spend time inside the minds of others. Leavitt has spent hours imagining herself "as someone trapped in the World Trade Center, or as a duchess on her wedding day, or as a friend who has lost a child, or as a homeless boy, a teenaged prostitute, a pioneer, or a prisoner."[8]

Habit #2: Take Notes

Once while in graduate school I volunteered to pick up author David Shields from the Columbus, Ohio, airport and drive him back to Athens where he was slated to give a reading. Hoping to make the most of a ninety-minute road trip with an author I admired, I spent the solitary drive to Columbus mulling over questions I might ask him. But once I picked Shields up, he spent much of the drive interviewing me.

He asked about my family, school, and my current projects, and though I managed enough questions to show I was interested in his life, he seemed doubly interested in mine. And I might have chalked that up to the skills of a good mentor but for the notebook he kept open the entire drive. He called to mind the image of a lanky gumshoe journalist, his long limbs folded into the front seat of my Ford Escort, a notebook propped on his knee, pen flying. After a good hour of him playing stenographer to our small talk, I finally asked him about the notebook. "I try to write down everything that might be useful later," he said. I remember feeling mildly flattered, but it also called to mind the slogan on a T-shirt I'd seen someone wearing at a conference earlier that year—"Be nice to me, or you might end up in my next book." The lesson here, of course, is that all the observations in the world won't help us if we don't write them down (and maybe a secondary lesson is that a serious writer keeps a notebook and pen handy, no matter what).

"If you are a writer, or want to be a writer, this is how you spend your days," writes Anne Lamott. "Listening, observing, storing things away, making your isolation pay off. You take home all you've taken in, all that you've overheard, and you turn it into gold. (Or at least you try.)"[9] Perhaps a tertiary lesson from Shields is that note-taking is idiosyncratic. I'm not a pen-and-paper guy like he is, but I use the Notes app in my smartphone compulsively. In the end, how we make notes is less important than our commitment to becoming what Natalie Goldberg describes as "a carrier of details that make up history."[10]

Habit #3: Write All the Time

If cultivating a habit of observation and note-taking is, in part, about treating every experience as a potential source of inspiration, then this third

NOTES ON NOTE-TAKING

"TRY TO BE ONE OF THE PEOPLE ON WHOM NOTHING IS LOST." - HENRY JAMES

MINIMUM INVESTMENT
FOR MAXIMUM FREEDOM

THE CHEAP & EASY APPROACH

"YOU SHOULD FEEL THAT YOU HAVE PERMISSION TO
WRITE THE WORST JUNK IN THE WORLD AND IT WOULD
BE OKAY . . . A CHEAP SPIRAL NOTEBOOK LETS YOU FEEL
THAT YOU CAN FILL IT QUICKLY AND AFFORD ANOTHER."
– NATALIE GOLDBERG

THE TYPE-A APPROACH

A JOURNAL
FOR WHAT HAPPENS
ON THE DAILY

A WRITING NOTEBOOK
FOR PROJECT SKETCHES,
LISTS, AND IDEAS

A PLANNER
TO TRACK PROGRESS
AND GOALS

"MY NOTEBOOKS KEEP ME WRITING - THROUGH REJECTION, TRIUMPH,
INSPIRATION, AND DISENCHANTMENT; IN THE FACE OF PRESCHOOLER TWINS,
TANTRUMS, FIELD TRIPS, AND SNOW DAYS; ON THE CRESTS AND IN THE
TROUGHS; AT HOME AND AWAY - ALL THE MONTHS OF THE YEAR."
– RANDON BILLINGS NOBLE

THE DIGITAL APPROACH

1. RECORD DAILY NOTES
AND OBSERVATIONS ON
A SMARTPHONE.

2. EVERY FEW DAYS, TRANSFER THE
GOOD STUFF TO A WORD DOC
(DON'T FORGET TO DATE THEM)

3. USE THE "SEARCH" FUNCTION
TO FIND ANYTHING, AND SAVE
IT FOREVER!

"IT'S ABOUT HAVING A DAILY OR WEEKLY PRACTICE OF RECORDING NOT JUST
THINGS YOU NOTICE, BUT THINGS THAT YOU'RE THINKING ABOUT, AND OBSESSED
WITH. THOSE ARE THE THINGS THAT OFTEN DEVELOP INTO BIGGER PROJECTS."
– TONI JENSEN

FIGURE 1 *"Notes on Note-Taking," with an epigraph from Henry James, "The Art of Fiction,"* Longman's Magazine 4 *(September 1884), March 1, 2022, https://public .wsu.edu/~campbelld/amlit/artfiction.html.*

habit is about treating every instance of writing as a creative opportunity. Every email, office memo, expense report, or term paper can be a practice session for mastering the sentence, for playing with prosody, and putting a little of ourselves on the page.

For students, this may seem like an easy proposition. At some point during my junior year of college, it occurred to me that no matter what class I was taking, I could treat each writing assignment like a creative project. Not that I began slipping iambs into my anthropology lecture notes or crafting vivid scenes in lab reports (that would be ridiculous), but I realized that every writing assignment needed a voice on the page and that I might as well cultivate that voice as my own. With a small, but crucial, mental shift like this, any writing assignment can become a chance to improve our craft.

Even if we're not in school, life can serve as a writing laboratory of its own. Work-related writing, social media posts, emails to family, and even text messages can serve as practice. After all, what's more refreshing than discovering a personality on the page where you would least expect it? Consider a few of my favorite examples:

Ms. Personality

Heather Hammond is the business manager in the English department where I teach, and part of her job includes sending out long, detailed emails to the entire faculty. It's often a thankless job, but she does it with a delightful sense of voice. In a recent email reminder about completing faculty reports, Hammond writes:

> Annual Reports are due Friday, January 15th. One might wonder if I'm really going to download these reports on Friday night instead of waiting until the following Tuesday after the holiday weekend. Your educated guess is probably correct.[11]

And in an email announcing a scheduled fire drill one winter morning, she included the subject line "Save Yourselves!" and wrote:

> Join me TODAY at our designated gathering location at 2:00 pm when our building goes up in imaginary flames. Bring your own coat and hot chocolate. I'll bring the snack. Last one there's a rotten egg.[12]

Hammond allows her personality to come through in her day-to-day correspondence without distracting from the content. That extra effort makes her emails a pleasure to read, and it elevates the act of memo writing to an art form.

Revenge of the Textbook Authors

There's not a lot of room in math and science textbooks for creative flourish, but many textbook writers have found that even a small gesture toward personality can mean a lot to readers. Take *University Physics with Modern Physics*, written by Hugh D. Young and Roger Freedman, which reads about the way you would imagine except for the occasional mention of a fictional character named *Cousin Throckmorton*. "Throcky," as the text often calls him, shows up as a character in several story problems: "At a family picnic" one problem reads, "you are appointed to push your obnoxious cousin Throckmorton in a swing."[13] Another reads, "Cousin Throckmorton holds one end of the clothesline taut and wiggles it up and down."[14] In each instance, Cousin Throckmorton induces a chuckle and infuses the problem with a little humanity.

And Throcky isn't the only example of textbook personality out there. A frightening, though unnamed, group of political science majors appear as characters in *Fundamentals of Physics* by David Halliday, Robert Resnick, and Jearl Walker. The question reads, in part:

> You are kidnapped by political-science majors (who are upset because you told them political science is not a real science). Although blindfolded, you can tell the speed of their car (by the whine of the engine), the time of travel (by mentally counting off seconds), and the direction of travel (by turns along the rectangular street system).[15]

Besides ascribing Jason Bourne-level survival skills to physics students, the question wants to know how far the kidnappers have driven and what direction the car is facing at the end of the drive.

Roger Freedman tells me that most contemporary physics textbooks contain similar playfulness. To Freedman and other writers, these creative choices are more than mere Easter eggs for overworked physics students— they're demonstrations of textual ownership, and according to Freedman, they remind students about the real-world implications of what they're studying. "It's important for students, who are often encountering physics for the first time, to recognize it as a human activity,"[16] says Freedman. A character such as Throckmorton reminds students that all those complex explanations and formulas have meaning in the real world and that beneath the surface of the text there's a real human being helping them figure things out.

Delight at the Museum

A few years ago, at the tail end of a study abroad trip, my family and I toured Cawdor Castle in Northern Scotland. We'd already done our share of ogling antiques in museums across the UK, and we thought we knew what to expect—lots of gilded-frame oil paintings, ornate porcelain dinnerware, and the high polish of spindly wooden furniture. But what we found on our tour of Cawdor took us completely by surprise.

The rooms themselves weren't all that unique (plenty of gilded-frame portraits and opulent furniture to go around), but in each room we discovered a plaque on the wall that included notes about the various items on display. Not the dry stuff of typical museum copy, but cheeky, sarcastic notes written by the 6th Earl of Cawdor himself.

In one room, a note about a pair of four-poster beds reads: "The beds are not identical twins, but even so, together, they form an undistinguished, amiable English couple."[17] In the updated kitchen, the Earl calls our attention to the modern copper range hood and points out how the ductwork exits "direct into the old chimney, removing the smell of haggis."[18] He refers to a medieval drinking horn as likely "a splendid and complete fake,"[19] the blade of an antique Persian knife as so blunt it "could scarcely cut a wedge of yoghurt,"[20] and a 4,000-year-old piece of Bronze Age stonework as an "incredibly boring lump of rock."[21]

The Earl's witty approach to what could have been a perfunctory catalog of family heirlooms and minor national treasures transformed our visit into what felt like a personalized tour with the Earl himself. And I'm all but certain the Earl had more fun with the work than if he'd stuck to standard museum expectations.

Habit #4: Be Intentional Online

For a writer in the developed world with relative income security and the time to put thoughts on paper, online distraction may be the single largest obstacle to good work. We tweet, share, scroll, click "Watch Next Episode," and largely ignore the fact that we all hold in our pockets access to the sum of all human intellectual, artistic, and scientific progress.

For all its potential as a resource, the Internet is ultimately a giant time-sucking void that traps us in dopamine feedback loops and keeps us from the most valuable work we can do as writers. Technologist Jaron Lanier refers to smartphones as "the cage that goes everywhere with you" and maintains that we should all get rid of social media because its "constant, subtle manipulation" is "unethical, cruel, dangerous, and inhuman."[22] Whether that's an overstatement or not, most of us would agree that when we go online we end up spending more time than we'd like performing the mental equivalent of cleaning lint from our belly buttons.

If we are to write well, we must ask ourselves hard questions about our Internet usage, and how it jibes with our writing goals. What are we reading? Who are we communicating with and why? How do we feel after killing time online? And if, after some thought, we decide we could use an intervention, there are a few ways to break out of the cage.

Software programs such as Cold Turkey, Freedom, and Serene, or browser plug-ins such as Self Control (on Chrome) or Impulse Blocker (on FireFox) can help stake out dedicated writing sessions by cutting off access to the Internet or other applications. Likewise, word processing programs such as Microsoft Word, Scrivener, Pages, and OpenOffice have "focus" and "full screen" modes that help eliminate distractions from a computer display. I've tried putting my phone in another room, or turning it off completely, but I prefer Francesco Cirillo's "Pomodoro" technique of muting my phone for a series of twenty-five-minute focused writing sessions.[23] After twenty-five minutes of writing, I get a five-minute break and then set the timer and go again.

And while it's nice to imagine that writerly productivity is simply a matter of downloading the right time management software, the truth is that to keep the Internet from interfering with our creative lives, we have to renegotiate our relationship with it all the time. One way we do that is by considering what being online really means. Sure we watch videos and scroll through endless images, but ultimately being online means reading and writing—a lot. And whether all that helps us become better writers will depend on how intentional we can be.

Read with Purpose

Scrolling a social media feed is such a passive experience that it seems hardly fair to call it reading (consider that word: *feed*. The Internet wants us to eat, but it wants to choose the meal and then force it down our throats). I might see a post from friends or from a few authors I know, and I'll definitely see plenty of advertisements, but no matter how interesting the link, I rarely click on it just in case something *more* interesting might be waiting farther down my screen.

Social media makes me feel like an awkward guest at a dinner party. Scrolling a feed is the social equivalent of sitting on the couch and listening as people walk by in conversation. It feels good to be in such thought-provoking, entertaining, and distracting company, and I know there's a conversation I want to get in on, but there are so many to choose from. A half-hour might go by and I'm still sitting on the couch having talked to no one. I've passed over chats with friends about their new job or their new pet or their trip to Florida, and I've passed over a conversation about a recent NPR story, and, oh hey, isn't that a famous author I admire? And I just read her book; I could go talk to her. But what if someone even better comes along? I'll just stay here on the couch.

This all adds up to a conviction that most of us are wasting the Internet as a text. Could we, in the time typically eaten up by scrolling through social media, engage instead with the work of individual writers—their stories, their poems and essays, their articles and opinion pieces? Are we groping in the darkness, hoping the machine of the Internet feeds us something worth reading all while missing the double pleasure of seeking out something beautiful and seeing how a skilled writer made it happen?

If I follow Joyce Carol Oates on Twitter, my feed gets the occasional treat of a book recommendation from the author, some smart political commentary, and the occasional video clip of a cat reciting Victorian love poetry. Alternatively, I could visit the author's web page,[24] and find short stories, interviews, craft essays, scholarly research, and novel excerpts. Should I follow JCO on Twitter? Probably (and I do), but would my writing life be better off if I spent more time on her website instead of on her Twitter feed? Definitely. And that doesn't even factor in the vast library of magazines, anthologies, journals, and literary sites at our fingertips when we sit with our phone in our hands.

Let's be realistic though. Few of us are going to quit social media altogether, but if we're intentional about our online reading, we can begin to treat the Internet less like a series of headlines ticking across that giant screen in Time Square and more like an empty bookshelf waiting to be filled.

Write with Urgency

Think about the types of text we write online. Heather Hammond has already helped us reconsider emails, but we can be intentional with all our online writing, from social media posts and comments to product reviews, blogs, and even fiction. Let's consider Annie Dillard for a moment. "Write as if you were dying," she tells us. "At the same time, assume you write for an audience consisting solely of terminal patients. What would you begin writing if you knew you would die soon? What could you say to a dying person that would not enrage by its triviality?"[25] Dillard wrote that in 1989, before most of us could imagine the Internet, let alone the trivialities that overwhelm us every time we log in. But her words have proven prophetic. "If [the writer] has ever bought a hamburger, or taken a commercial airplane flight, she spares her readers a report of her experience."[26] What might we spare our readers on the social media channels and comment threads of the Internet? What might we post if our friends and followers knew we were dying, or if we knew they were dying? And if we find ourselves saying, *But wait, this is just the Internet. If I were dying, I wouldn't be spending all my time online*, then perhaps that in itself is an answer.

Then again, we can find authors using social media in thoughtful, expressive ways that enhance both their own writing lives and the larger literary experience of the Internet. Consider journalist Jeff Sharlet, author of, among other books, *The Brilliant Darkness*, which grew out of a series of photographs and captions posted to Instagram. While in a funk about the value of his work as a journalist, and in the wake of his father's heart attack, Sharlet began making regular late night drives from his home in Vermont over the Green Mountains to his father's home in Schenectady, New York. Sharlet started taking photos of night shift workers he met along the way and learning their stories. "I thought I was just taking snapshots," he writes. "And yet these snapshots, and the questions I asked, and other people's answers, seemed to me, in the middle of the night to matter more than the work I'd been publishing as journalism." For Sharlet, posting his photos and collected stories to Instagram felt, he says, "like the first story I'd ever written. As if I were only now, in the long night between my father's home and mine, becoming a writer."[27]

Sharlet reminds us that social media can be a home for more than our political rants and vacation photos. That, as writers, we can turn online forums into literary spaces in which to examine our own humanity, embrace our individual vulnerability and discover a world of new stories to tell.

To Blog or Not to Blog

Social media aside, the Internet offers plenty of purpose-built venues for flexing our creative writing muscles. Take blogging, for instance. The blogosphere used to feel like the Wild West of the Internet—raw, unfiltered, unpolished, idiosyncratic, and often quite self-absorbed. But over the past two decades, blogging has become a slick, polished cog in a machine that the business world calls "content marketing." Every organization from the White House to Pornhub has a blog. Blogging services such as WordPress, Medium, Substack, and others are constantly expanding possibilities for writers. There are food blogs and sports blogs; tech blogs and marketing blogs; and so, so many blogs about making blogs. Some have become important sources of niche information, and some are little more than vessels for advertising and search engine optimization.

But from the standpoint of creative composition, the value of a personal blog hasn't changed much since writers first started using them at the beginning of the twenty-first century. At their most basic, personal blogs offer a space to share work, the possibility of reader feedback, and an easy way to increase writerly discipline. "If you blog every day, you're in effect practicing your craft," writes self-publishing guru Steven Spatz. And he also likes blogging for the potential access to feedback. Not just "from well-meaning family members who might hold back, but from real life readers who will respond generally to the different styles and strokes you play with." If we're lucky enough to have real readers, that kind of feedback can be invaluable, but the public aspect of blogging can also be problematic if it becomes an end in itself. "Good writing takes time," writes Spatz. "And the ease of blogging and sharing can subvert the process of getting to your best content."[28]

Fan Fiction for All

Perhaps the most famous work to come from fan fiction is E. L. James's *50 Shades of Gray* trilogy, which made so much money and garnered so much attention that it has become regular practice for certain publishers to scour fan-fiction sites for the next Anastasia Steele and Christian Gray. Sites such as fan-fiction.net, wattpad.com, and archiveofourown.org provide platforms for millions of writers of all ages and backgrounds to create, share, and consume stories based on characters from movies, television, books, comics, video games, and, most curious to me, musicians and music groups (Taylor Swift and One Direction are apparently popular subjects).

Fan fiction has a lot to offer as a writing environment. First, community is relatively easy to find. B. Zelkovich, a fan-fiction writer and reader since her teens, got her first real attention as a writer in a fan-fiction community: "After years of writing fiction in a vacuum, where the only feedback was found in classroom workshops, reading comments on my fic felt like stepping out into the first rays of summer sun." In a short time, she "went from the solitary writer, alone in her study, to a content creator people . . . recognized and enjoyed interacting with."[29]

Such interaction can be an ego boost for sure, but it's more than that. As Julie Beck explains in *The Atlantic*, "In these online communities, writers of all ages and skill levels . . . are learning and teaching others how to write, and write well."[30] Scholars Katie Davis and Cecilia Aragon describe the process as "distributed mentoring," where fan-fiction writers benefit from "a complex, reciprocal network of advice."[31] Because fan-fiction writers are also fan-fiction readers, participants engage in a web of commentary that can't help but improve the writing of everyone involved.

For all the clear benefits of fan fiction, there are some notes of caution as well. In her most productive fan-fiction year, Zelkovich wrote more than 200,000 words. She calls it "the most output I've ever had in any writing capacity," but it came at the expense of her deeper, more personal goals as a writer. "I also didn't get anything done on my own content hardly at all."[32] Balance was an issue for Zelkovich, and there's also the question of who fan fiction authors are working for. As critic Stephanie Burt explains, "No clearer path from new writers to potentially interested readers has existed in the history of civilization," but that audience is a "wholly voluntary, non-paying" group of people who dig fan fiction because it depicts "characters that other people already recognize, characters whose further adventures other people already want to read."[33] So while inhabiting the worlds and characters of others may help us improve our writing, there's a real opportunity cost to spending our creative energy exploring and expanding the worlds of others while ignoring our own.

In the end, I'm reluctant to be too prescriptive about how a writer should spend their time online. As Jaron Lanier writes, "You can't use the internet well until you've confronted it on your own terms."[34] How we fortify ourselves against the temptations and distractions of the information age is by necessity a personal choice; how we engage on social media and how much we invest in an online presence via blogs or fan fiction are up to each of us to decide. But it's worth quoting Jonathan Franzen here, who, in his curmudgeonly way, reminds us that the instant access to audience and feedback can distract us from the purpose of art. "It's not like I'm militantly opposed to discursive interactive communication," he told *Salon* back in 2013. "It's fine, it's great. But there's a tipping point you reach where you can't get away from the electronic community, where you become almost physically dependent on it. And that, I persist in thinking, is not compatible with my notion of where terrific literature comes from."[35] Our success as writers will hinge a great deal on using the Internet well, and unless we take the time to consider how the Internet is affecting our writing life, our response to the pull of the Internet will hardly be a choice at all.

IS THERE ULTIMATELY A trick to making the most of our daily lives as writers? Sure, if you describe being ready for experience and inspiration wherever and whenever it comes, as a "trick." Life will happen whether or not we're paying attention, but approaching each day with an open mind and pen in hand will help us take note, so to speak. "Writing is a tool that enables people in every discipline to wrestle with facts and ideas," writes William Zinsser. "It compels us by the repeated effort of language to go after those thoughts and to organize them and present them clearly."[36] The more intentional we are with every act of reading and writing, and the more wholeheartedly we commit to the "repeated effort of language," the more you and I can turn the mundane toil of the everyday into a laboratory for writerly improvement.

2.

MASTERING THE ART OF THE WRITING GROUP

At a writing conference in San Antonio, Texas, I sat in a seminar room and listened to Kenyan College professor Ira Sukrungruang describe one of his worst days as a new creative writing teacher. "It was my first workshop ever," he said. "I must have been twenty-two years old. It was a night class, and most of my students were older than me." The students had spent the first half of the semester discussing model texts and then each signed up to share their own work.

The first student to share was a woman Sukrungruang described as "talkative" and "always on top of class discussions." Her early assignments had been fine, so he had no reason to suspect that her workshop would be any different.

"As soon as she came into the room, I knew something was off," he continued. Where earlier she'd been lighthearted and sarcastic, she now sat quietly, staring at the floor. And then, as the discussion began, things turned sour. In response to every critical comment, the student let out a sigh or rolled her eyes dramatically. "At one point, she began strumming her fingers on the desk in a loud, exaggerated way," said Sukrungruang. "I knew something was wrong, but I let it go. I didn't know what else to do." Then one student, a young man that Sukrungruang described as "among the more socially caustic students in the classroom," opened his mouth. "He didn't say anything outside the bounds of appropriate criticism, but it was the last straw. The author got up from her chair, walked to the middle of the circle, and gave a spinning double middle finger to the entire classroom, and then she ran out.[1]

Joining a writing group, whether a formal university course or a casual gathering of friends, is a signal to the world that we're ready to take our work seriously. It's also a signal that we're willing to fail. For, as Sukrungruang's story highlights, an essential tension in all writing groups is the potential for failure. In the best groups, such potential helps foster a sense of collective vulnerability and encourages a mutual sense of responsibility to one another's work. I call this the golden rule of writing groups—critique unto others as you would have them critique unto you. In the best writing groups, we listen, take notes, ask questions, and check our own biases in order to help each author fulfill their own vision. As a result, we cultivate courage to take risks, we develop thicker skin in the face of criticism, produce more interesting work, and find support from a group of writers invested in mutual success.

In the worst writing groups though, potential for failure can provoke defensiveness, competition, jealousy, and, occasionally, obscene hand gestures of impressive acrobatic complexity. In the worst writing groups, we show up to hear ourselves talk. We jockey for position as the best writer in the room, and we clumsily impose our preconceived notions of literature on everyone else. As a result, we avoid risk, take criticism personally, produce derivative work, and ultimately find ourselves hobbled by the tyranny of consensus.

In reality, most writing groups land somewhere in the middle of these two extremes—a handful of imperfect individuals burdened with our own prejudices and predispositions, alive with our own hopes and fears about our work, each of us banking on the group to help us discover what we really want to say. It's a lot to ask from a few friends sitting around a table in some coffee shop, let alone a bunch of strangers in a classroom.

Here's the uncomfortable truth, though: a writing group is only as good as its least prepared members. Consider Sukrungruang's story again. The workshop didn't fail because of overly critical students. It failed because one student didn't know how to handle critique. So whether we're gearing up for our first formal workshop experience as part of a university creative writing program or we're preparing a manuscript to submit to an informal group of friends, it falls on each of us to understand the nature of the writing groups we're in and be ready to do our part.

Formal Writing Workshops

What might we need to know about the history of the university creative writing workshop in order to be a responsible member of one? It may help to know that the University of Iowa is traditionally seen as the birthplace of the creative writing program—a discipline that grew out of a larger humanistic effort in early twentieth-century higher education to study literature in ways that make us better thinkers, better writers, and better people.[2] It may also help to know that the classroom approach wherein a student-author sits quietly and listens as others review their manuscript is called "The Iowa Model" and is the most common form of writing workshop in the United States.

Beyond those basics, it might also help to know that plenty of writers have some beef with the workshop model. In his well-known editorial for *The New Yorker* "MFA vs POC," Junot Diaz details complaints about the university creative writing experience that have been echoed by many writers of color. As Diaz points out, the creative writing workshop has historically been and continues to be, a predominately white space, where white teachers and white students discuss the work of white authors in a white cultural context, and, as a result writers of color have often felt excluded, tokenized, or otherwise marginalized in the workshop environment. "Simply put," writes Diaz, "I was a person of color in a workshop whose theory of reality did not include my most fundamental experiences as a person of color—that did not in other words include me."[3]

And similar concerns have been raised by members of other traditionally underrepresented groups. Freelance writer Jen Corrigan describes the way her "angry" writing is often received in workshop by male colleagues. "As a woman, I am allowed to . . . write about the injustices done to me, but only if I write about those experiences passively . . . to actively point a finger at the men who have harmed me is somehow crossing the line."[4] Ana Valens, a transgender freelance journalist, describes having to teach herself how to write LGBTQ characters. "As an English major who learned the craft through creative writing courses, I was never taught how to write about the [LGBTQ] community."[5] And University of Memphis MFA graduate Alyssa Radtke, who has cerebral palsy, describes the pressure she felt from fellow workshop members to be a spokesperson for her disability. "I get asked about how I have sex more often than I get asked about how I avoid blood clots when I sit for such long periods. Both are private matters, though people feel entitled to answers regardless."[6]

To these voices add a legion of scholars, teachers, and artists who have raised questions about the pedagogical and aesthetic value of the university workshop. Rosalie Morales Kearns, pointing to the Iowa Model, warns that silencing authors risks turning the workshop into a "bullying session" wherein any deviation from aesthetic norms is automatically labeled as a mistake "rather than a deliberate artistic choice."[7] And all these concerns may be summed up by the venerable poet Donald Hall, who has compared the university creative writing workshop to a fast-food kitchen where "the good old McPoem" waits "on the steam shelf for us, wrapped and protected, indistinguishable, undistinguished," at the mercy of what he calls "the quality control of the least common denominator."[8]

In the face of such skepticism, we may wonder why the workshop model continues to thrive. One answer might be that for all its shortcomings the workshop has been for many of us an invaluable resource, especially early in our careers. Reading assignments and accompanying discussions have helped introduce us to model texts. Writing prompts have encouraged our creativity and taught us to think and compose like experienced writers. And, most importantly, peer review has allowed us to engage with an audience when the stakes are relatively low. Given the ubiquitous nature and potential value of the workshop, it's a good idea to figure out what we can do to make the most of it.

The Curriculum

A typical creative writing curriculum can be divided into four categories: reading and discussing model texts, completing generative writing exercises, meeting one-on-one with an instructor, and engaging in both small group and class-wide peer review. And while each is important, what we get from them ultimately depends on our preparation and willingness to engage.

Reading assignments: These can be discouragingly homogenous (often a bunch of dead white dudes) or delightfully diverse. They can represent the old standards of the traditional canon (also often a bunch of dead white dudes) or they can cover an eclectic assortment of voices from across the social and cultural spectrum. But whatever a reading list looks like, our job is to read it. This may seem obvious, but anyone who has taught a creative writing course can recall the painful torture of sitting in a room full of students who haven't done the reading.

To Dr. Sarah Jefferis, reading is an essential part of the creative process. "Writers need to read about other people's experiences that are not their own," says Jefferis. "If a white male poet from New England has only ever read Robert Frost, then they haven't done much to expand their frame of reference."[9] Just reading, though, isn't enough. How we read matters. I like Robert Pinsky's advice to "read the way a cook eats,"[10] but any number of metaphors will do. Read the way a mechanic listens to an engine; the way a doctor sounds the palpitations of the heart or the way a rock climber maps the face of a cliff. Pay attention to the seduction of words, to the rhythm of sentences, to the scaffolding of structure. Note the composition of beginnings, the harmonies of theme, and the resonance of endings. Reading in workshop is about learning to recognize the expectations a text establishes for itself and how it fulfills those expectations. In short, we ought to ask ourselves how an author, armed only with the tools of diction, syntax, rhythm, metaphor, imagery, allusion, and imagination can speak to us from across the great divide of time, space, and the limits of human empathy.

Generative writing: Informal writing activities are staples of the creative writing classroom. An instructor may ask us to complete a daily journal or start each class period by responding to a prompt. Some instructors play music. Others turn the lights down. One teacher I know begins writing sessions by ringing a meditation gong. The goal, as Wendy Bishop describes it, is for students to leave the classroom each day with "a discovery or a surprise that will lead [them] into productive out-of-class writing."[11]

At the very least, prompts can help purge our subpar writing. "Most of us are full up with bad stories, boring stories, self-indulgent stories, searing works of unendurable melodrama," writes novelist Ann Patchett. "We must get all of them out of our system in order to find the good stories that may or may not exist in the freshwater underneath."[12] We might also consider how a prompt can help us generate ideas for larger assignments in the course.

Often instructors will ask students to share their responses with one another. This is a chance to shut our notebooks, listen, and make note of language that inspires us. And then when it's our turn to read, we skip the apologies and read what we've written—even just a sentence or two. The small graces we offer one another in such a setting will pay dividends when the time comes to share more polished manuscripts.

Instructor conferences: An instructor may require one-on-one consultations, or we may have to reach out on our own, but either way, receiving feedback outside of formal grading situations is important. Creative writing instructors are experienced editors and readers, and they can be an excellent sounding board for our ideas. In my own workshops, the students who write the most compelling work are the students who share their progress with me on a regular basis.

Before meeting with an instructor, email them a manuscript, and prepare some specific questions. "Can you recommend some extra reading that might help me get a handle on writing unreliable narrators" is a better question than "Who are your favorite authors?" And "I don't know how to end this sonnet" is a better starter than "What's wrong with my poem?" Then, if an instructor offers advice, give it real consideration. Even if we don't end up applying a particular suggestion, trying out the advice of a seasoned writer can help us see our own projects more clearly.

Submitting to Workshop

Sharing manuscripts in a class-wide workshop can be the most rewarding part of a creative writing course, but as I've already said, the quality of the workshop depends on the commitment of its individual members. For those submitting work, keep in mind the following advice:

Prepare: Submit a work in progress, but do not submit something totally new. "First drafts are too undeveloped and scattered to be productively critiqued in a group setting," writes novelist Jim Nelson. On the other hand, "late drafts are usually too set in concrete."[13] The sweet spot lies somewhere beyond that first draft where we've written our hearts out and aren't sure where to go next. Ideally, we've let the manuscript sit for a day or two and then come back to it at least one more time before sharing it with others. Also, take formatting seriously. Skip the plastic document covers and colored fonts, but give some thought to a title, typeface, the use of white space, and headings. Include page numbers, and double-space the text for easy reading. When we treat our own manuscript with the respect it deserves, our classmates are more likely to do the same.

Ask for specific help: We should have some idea of where we want a manuscript to go and what might be keeping it from getting there. Even if we don't, we ought to at least have some questions for our readers. "When I run a workshop," writes Eastern Washington University professor Rachel Toor, "no one—including me—is allowed to say 'I want' about someone else's writing. It's not about what you want . . . It's about what the writer is trying to do and how you can help."[14] And our readers will have an easier time helping if we share our goals and questions upfront.

Welcome criticism: If we think of critique as part of the writing process (and not as some examination we either pass or fail), we're more likely to take that criticism well. Our readers are doing us a favor, and they deserve our gratitude and patience: gratitude for their time and attention and patience with their imperfections or unintentional insensitivities. Some readers will have more writing experience. Some may understand our goals more clearly. Some may have better knowledge of the cultural context we're working from. Others may not. Regardless, criticism of all kinds offers us a chance to reflect on our work and to approach it with a more objective eye—and for that we can be grateful.

Final Portfolio

Most workshops end with submitting some kind of final portfolio—a collection of our revised work meant to demonstrate our growth over the course of a semester. Successful students use these portfolios to try out major revisions. They don't merely look at comments from instructors and classmates and follow the majority opinion. Instead, they pore over feedback and use it to develop their own revision plan. Most instructors would rather have a student take a big swing in revision and miss than play it safe with a few tweaks here and there and hope for a decent grade.

And finally, if an instructor takes the time to leave feedback on a portfolio, don't abandon it to rot in your email inbox or the instructor's filing cabinet. Treat the portfolio as just another step in the writing process. Collect the feedback, let it sit for a few days or weeks, and then go back to it and see what there is to learn.

What to Do when It's All Over

What happens after a semester ends will depend on how well we internalize the lessons of the creative writing workshop. Have we learned to read carefully with an ear for effect? Have we learned to rely on great works of literature for inspiration? Have we developed a habit of daily writing? Are we better at giving and receiving feedback? Do we see ourselves as writers with goals and the tools to achieve them? If we can answer yes to even a few of those questions, then the workshop will have done its job.

Of course, university creative writing workshops are short lived, and amid the chaos and distraction of everyday life, keeping up good habits can be difficult. That is why informal writing groups can be such an important tool in helping us maintain the writing life.

Informal Writing Groups

Gathering to share work with a few friends can provide many of the same benefits as a formal workshop but requires more planning and commitment to sustain (no one's paying tuition, after all). If we're thinking about organizing such a group, there are a few things we can do to increase our chances of success.

Find the Right Partners

If we're already in a formal writing workshop, it may not be hard to talk a few classmates into carrying on a writing group when the semester is over, but it doesn't take a formal group to start an informal one. First, look local. Chances are that someone from work, book club, church, or that weekend LARPING collective is also working on a novel or sitting on a batch of poems they've never shared with anyone. Writers are everywhere, and it just takes a motivated somebody to gather a few of them into a room, lay down some ground rules, and get writing.

The Internet also offers access to an expansive literary community. Just Google "Facebook Writing Group" and see what comes up. Of course, not all online communities will be a good fit, so do some research. Lurk a bit on various sites, look for writers with similar interests, and find out the protocol for sharing work. Always volunteer to read for someone else before asking for help.

Remember too that it's okay to be picky. Just because our college roommate or sister-in-law wants to join our writing group doesn't mean we should let them. Rachel Toor describes allowing others to see our unfinished work as the "intellectual equivalent of sorting through our dirty laundry,"[15] which means we want people we trust to do the sorting. Writing partners should have serious writing goals, whether personal or professional. They should be writers whose work we admire—otherwise how will we trust their advice? And, of course, if we're pals that helps too, but feedback that's honest should be a priority over feedback that's friendly.

Choose the Right Size

Claire P. Curtis, professor of political science at Charleston College, has participated in writing groups for years, and for her, three is the magic number. "Three gives enough people to have useful assessments, without too much disparate advice. Three keeps you focused, and three means the members of the group—like the legs on a stool—will keep it up and going."[16] Perhaps the principle to remember is simply "keep it small." Too big and members may find it easier to bail out or leave others to carry the workload of critique.

Set a Schedule

Once a week? Once a month? Once a quarter? The bottom line: meet regularly, and keep the appointment sacred. "If it is your week to distribute writing, then you must circulate something," says Claire P. Curtis. "There is no backing out."[17] And, says novelist Xu Xi, "The only real rule is civility." Also consider having an appointed leader. "There has to be a central organizer who can help arrange the schedule, send out reminders, and help keep the group on task."[18] In some groups, everyone shares work at every meeting. In others, members take turns submitting. In some, manuscripts are shared ahead of time, while in others the first few minutes of each meeting are set aside for reading.

Make the Commitment

Formal writing workshops succeed because everyone has some skin in the game. Members are paying tuition or are otherwise enrolled in a program. Informal groups are only as strong as the commitment of the individual members. So make group expectations clear, and then make that time slot on the calendar sacred.

The Ethics of Critique

When we commit to a writing group or formal workshop, we also make a dual commitment to vulnerability and compassion. We commit to accepting questions, opinions, and criticism. But we also commit to considerate close reading and to checking our own aesthetic and cultural assumptions in favor of helping each author realize their own artistic vision.

Such a dual commitment should foster a mutual sense of responsibility and humility, especially given how deeply ingrained our own aesthetic and cultural assumptions can often be. But no matter our background or biases, it takes only a little forethought and intention to help create a space of inclusion, respect, and support.

Offer Compassionate Critique

In any writing group, we ought to keep in mind that authors are not writing for us, but rather we are reading for them. "You are there to help them do their best work—not their almost best work,"[19] says choreographer and art education pioneer Liz Lerman. But this can only happen in an environment of generous, compassionate critique. Not vapid praise or soft-gloved pandering, but selfless, heartfelt reactions and observations grounded in a desire to help the author realize their own vision. It takes time to learn how to offer this kind of critique, and it starts with remembering a few basic principles.

The first is to **resist the tendency to impose our own world view on a manuscript**. This means learning to recognize and check our biases as we read. We might find ourselves placing too much importance on our own experience:

That's never happened to me, so it must not be realistic
Wait, parts of this are in a foreign language?
That's not how a cop would talk

Or privileging our own aesthetic:

Narratives shouldn't break like this
Poetry shouldn't rhyme
There's too much research in this essay

Or prioritizing our own moral or social values:

> *This is too political*
> *This is too religious*
> *This is too graphic*

Often such opinions are born of discomfort. We read content that calls into question our personal values and beliefs, demands that we reconsider our own culpability in social ills, or breaks from our aesthetic norms, and we can feel tempted to label that discomfort as a problem. But as Rosalie Morales Kearns suggests, we ought to leave room for the possibility that such moves are an author's attempt to "disrupt reader expectations or experiment with something new."[20] Naga Noor and Robert McGill suggest that an inclusive writing group resists chalking up discomfort and confusion to an author's failings and instead considers "what purposes the production of confusion could serve, thus helping the writer to gauge how well their intended reactions have been achieved."[21]

Liz Lerman suggests that we "discover . . . the issue inside [our discomfort] and then turn that into a neutral question." Asking neutral questions takes the responsibility for the manuscript off the reader's shoulders and ensures that "the artist is doing the work trying to problem solve."[22]

So instead of saying *I don't think a cop would talk like that*, we can ask *How do you want this cop's dialog to influence the reader?* Instead of *there's too much research in this essay*, we can ask *What effect are you going for by including this research?* Instead of *this poem is too religious*, we can ask *How do you hope this poem is received by a secular audience?* Such questions can help mitigate some of the undue pressure our opinion can place on an author or their manuscript.

The second principle is that **praise is often as helpful, if not more helpful than criticism**. Too often writing groups are, as Goucher College professor Madison Smartt Bell describes it, "incapable of recognizing success." Too often they become a "fault-finding mechanism" designed to "diagnose and prescribe."[23] In addition to giving criticism, we can help authors recognize their strengths. Is a line of poetry particularly evocative? Let the author know why. Does a certain character charm or disgust? Help the author understand how their language induced that reaction. Sincere praise will be encouraging and can make it easier for the author to accept questions and criticism down the line.

Feedback of all kinds is more useful if it's backed up with specifics from the text, and that's our third principle: **Detailed critique**. It isn't enough to comment *I'm not sure this character is working*, or *this character is so relatable*. We have to get beneath the surface of such words. For instance, when we say a character is not *working*, we might mean that we're struggling to believe the character's motives, and when we say a character is *relatable*, we might mean that the combination of the character description and dialog

THE ART OF FEEDBACK

"RESERVING JUDGEMENTS IS A MATTER OF INFINITE HOPE."
— F. SCOTT FITZGERALD

INSTEAD OF: TRY THIS:

"I'M NOT SURE THIS CHARACTER IS WORKING."

"FOR THIS TO BE A SYMPATHETIC CHARACTER, WE MAY NEED TO KNOW MORE ABOUT HER MOTIVATIONS."

"I'M CONFUSED."

"I'M NOT CLEAR ON WHY THIS CHARACTER IS ANGRY. IS UNCERTAINTY PART OF WHAT YOU'RE GOING FOR?"

"I LOVE THIS LINE!"

"THE SYNCOPATED RHYTHM HERE IS REALLY SATISFYING."

"YOUR ENDING COULD USE SOME WORK."

"WHAT IS THE IDEA YOU HOPE TO LEAVE WITH A READER BY ENDING THE WAY YOU HAVE?"

"SO RELATABLE."

"THIS SCENE PAINTS SUCH A CLEAR PICTURE OF A 1980'S CHILDHOOD IN THE MIDWEST."

"WHAT'S GOING ON HERE?"

"WHAT IS THE LOGIC THAT'S GUIDING THE ARRANGEMENT OF THESE FRAGMENTS?"

FIGURE 2 *"The Art of Feedback," with an epigraph from F. Scott Fitzgerald,* The Great Gatsby, *Project Gutenberg, March 1, 2022, https://www.gutenberg.org/files /64317/64317-h/64317-h.htm.*

helps create a clear image of the character's personality in our mind. But if we aren't specific and detailed with our critique, we leave the author guessing at what exactly they've done right.

Avoid Turning Writers into "Native Informants"

As much as our writing is influenced by our sociocultural, religious, ethnic, and racial backgrounds, Noor and McGill warn that inclusive writing groups must avoid "creating an explicit or implicit expectation" that writers become spokespersons for their race or culture. An Asian American writer, for instance, should not be expected to write only about Asian American life nor to speak for all Asian Americans. Nor should a writer with disabilities be expected to write only about disability or speak for all people with disabilities.

On the other hand, some writers may intentionally take on the mantle of native informant, and when they do we ought to help them prepare for the scrutiny that comes with it. As Noor and McGill explain, an inclusive workshop can help a writer "examine the grounds for their claims to cultural authority and to imagine challenges to their work."[24]

Respect Cultural Difference

As literary artists we should write what we need to write but also avoid exploiting, stereotyping, or othering cultures that are not our own. Svetlana Mintcheva, director of programs at the National Coalition Against Censorship, believes that "culture should be approached as complex systems rather than boutiques of exoticism offering ideas and practices ripped out of their cultural and historical context." But she's also wary of outright censorship: "We have a serious problem if the awareness of the pitfalls of trans-cultural borrowing is used to demand its absolute prohibition."[25]

What Mintcheva refers to here is the difference between cultural appropriation, which writer Jarune Uwujaren defines as "a centuries' old pattern of taking, stealing, exploiting, and misunderstanding the history and symbols that are meaningful to people of marginalized cultures,"[26] and cultural exchange—what Jezebel founder Anna Holmes calls "a certain sort of generosity, an openness to discussion and an invitation to reciprocity."[27]

While obvious instances of cultural exploitation are easy to identify (think of white performers in black face or a baseball team named "The Braves"), in literature such appropriation can be much more subtle. But as Anna Holmes writes, "Underlying the idea of appropriation is the sense that something—or someone—is just there for the taking: A style of dress, a personal narrative, an entire continent. You can't always prove appropriation. But you usually know it when you see it."[28] To that end,

I've compiled advice from several writers and critics that can help us see appropriation not only in the work of others but in our own work as well.

Behave like a guest (not a tourist or an invader): This comes from freelance writer Nisi Shawl who in turn attributes the idea to Diantha Day Sprouse. "Tourists are expected. They're generally a nuisance, but at least they pay their way," writes Shawl. Invaders, on the other hand, "arrive without warning, take whatever they want for use in whatever way they see fit." Better to be a guest, says Shawl. "Guests are invited. Their relationships with their hosts can become long-term commitments and are often reciprocal."[29]

Avoid "the salad bar" approach: Multimedia journalist Ixty Quintanilla says authors guilty of this approach find "an 'interesting' aspect of a culture, whether it be tattoos or a spiritual ceremony, and pluck it out of the entire community without any cultural context. This then creates a shallow, inaccurate, and insensitive representation of a community."[30]

Do the right kind of research: "Be aware of who wrote the books and articles you are reading," says novelist Jeannette Ng. "This isn't to say that only portraits from within a culture are accurate or insightful, but if your only sources are written by outsiders, then it is very easy to pick up those unconscious biases. There will be misconceptions that have been rattling around that literature for years because people are just citing each other in an echo chamber."[31]

Scrutinize motivations: Novelist Kit De Waal argues, "we have to ask ourselves who we are and what we are trying to say in speaking as 'the other.'" She suggests a series of questions: "What are we trying to accomplish in our writing that needs that perspective? Are we the best person to say it? ... Are we sure that we are not dabbling in exotica, in that fascination with the other that prevents us portraying a rounded, rich culture with all its nuances, diversity and reality? By writing our story are we taking the place of someone better placed to tell it?"[32]

Ask for help: YA novelist Julie Berry hires sensitivity readers to help her avoid appropriation. "There's no weakness or cowardice in acknowledging that you don't know what you don't know," writes Berry. "We all know how aggravating it is to see ourselves depicted in a way that's just a little bit off—gender, race, religion. As an artist I'd like to cause that experience to others as little as possible."[33] In the end though, we should not expect a sensitivity reader to catch all our cultural appropriation issues. We have to put in the work first and then ask for help.

"Cultural appropriation, at its root, is about power," writes novelist Balogun Ojetade. "Power to name; power to define."[34] When we write about a culture other than our own, we wield that power, and that can scare us into avoiding even the appearance of appropriation. But if we exercise some caution, behaving as a guest in another's culture, doing the right kind of research, examining our motives, and seeking help at the appropriate stage, we can write with the kind of humility and confidence we need to do our best work. As Mintcheva reminds us, "the ethical imperative is . . . to imagine responsibly and with empathy, not to avoid imagining at all."[35]

IN OUR EFFORT to create an inclusive writing group, we won't always get things right, but that's no reason to stop trying. Melissa Febos reminds us that the creative writing workshop "is the exact right place to make a mistake, because it's way easier to slip up here than when you're doing it out there on Twitter, or in a published work, where you can't take it back or revise it." And when mistakes are made, it's best to point them out immediately and without a lot of drama. "When we have people who mess up and show their biases or show their ignorance," says Febos, "I just tell them: 'Hey, this is a problem and let's fix it.'"[36] And that kind of direct approach is possible only if everyone in the workshop has embraced the dual commitment to compassion and vulnerability. It is through compassion that we can offer our fellow writers the benefit of the doubt as we kindly suggest changes. And it is vulnerability that helps us accept criticism and express gratitude to others for trying to help us do better. Certainly that's a tall order, but if we get it right then we do more than create a helpful writing group—we create a community.

3.

BECOMING A GOOD LITERARY CITIZEN

Years ago, I spent a tired afternoon staffing a booth for a literary magazine at a massive writing conference book fair. It was the last day of the conference, and after spending hours passing out flyers and talking with strangers, I was more than ready for the end of my shift. But then a woman approached, her arms full of books, busy in conversation with a friend at her side. Her name tag said "Patricia Smith," and I pulled a double take. "Patricia Smith?" I said. "You're Patricia Smith!?" I'd just read *Blood Dazzler*, her heartbreaking poetry collection about the people affected by Hurricane Katrina, and here she was, standing in front of me. I wanted to jump up and hug her, to grab someone from across the aisle and say, "Do you know who this is right here?"

I didn't jump up, but I did make a fool of myself. I gushed. I may have teared up. I told Smith how much I loved the book, that I was teaching it to my students, that I was so grateful she'd written it. I'm sure that people nearby looked at me the way people do when someone at the park starts monologuing to the pigeons. But I didn't care. Smith's book had moved me. And I wanted her to know.

Smith, for her part, was gracious. She thanked me, promised to send some poems to our magazine, and then walked away. And while she likely doesn't remember the exchange, I do, and not just for the fanboy absurdity of the moment. Creative writing is a large, motley community of free thinkers, activists, teachers, artists, and storytellers who are generally allergic to disingenuous attempts at calculated professional networking. Instead, writing communities thrive on a kind of reciprocal energy. We read something that moves us, and we want others to know about it. We share books like neighbors share recipes, we write fan mail and fan fiction, we post reviews and write critiques, we attend readings, we subscribe to literary magazines, and we write our own work in conversation with what we're reading.

Good literary citizenship means sharing and defending literary art not because it will be good for our careers but because all meaningful art needs champions. And perhaps, most importantly, it means remembering that behind every bit of literature is a real human being and that when we engage with literature, we're really engaging with one another. In practical terms, literary citizenship can mean reading outside our genre comfort zones in order to embrace a larger creative universe. It can mean attending (or even volunteering at) local literary events or maybe even sponsoring one ourselves. It can mean entering the public conversation to share informed opinions about what we're reading. Good literary citizenship starts with passion for literary art and ends when we find creative ways to celebrate and promote that art wherever we may find it.

Read across Boundaries of Genre and Culture

"You have to read widely," writes Stephen King. "Constantly refining (and redefining) your own work as you do so."[1] If we want to write space operas about mutant vampires, we better read a lot of space operas about mutant vampires. But reading is about more than finding models we can imitate. And it's about more than getting familiar with "the greats." If we want our work to expand beyond the narrow limits of our own experience and sociocultural boundaries, then our reading should also expand beyond those same narrow limits.

And let's not reduce such intentional diversification to mere political correctness. "It's about opening yourself to a multiplicity of perspectives," writes Roxane Gay. "We like what we like, and there's nothing wrong with that, but it never hurts to read beyond your comfort zone once in a while."[2] When we read beyond those comfort zones, we allow texts to challenge our preconceived notions of literature, and we affirm the value of cultures and experiences that differ from our own. If, for instance, I want to write sonnets, I better read my Shakespeare, but I probably ought to also read "Gay Chaps at the Bar" by Gwendolyn Brooks, *Love, Death and the Changing of the Seasons* by Marilyn Hacker, and "Tales from the Islands" by Derrick Walcott.

Why not mix up genres too? Certainly reading the novels of Colson Whitehead or the essays of Leslie Jamison will make me a more thoughtful, world-wise, empathetic poet. And reading the poetry of Jericho Brown or the plays of Tennessee Williams will help me produce fiction that captures more fully the gradations of the human experience. If I'm a slam poet, might I benefit from some Montaigne or Mailer? If a memoirist, then a little Basho or Bishop? If all I want to do is tell stories about mutant vampires in space, what comes from reading Jhumpa Lahiri, Cormac McCarthy, or Claudia Rankine?

When we read outside our pet genres and across the boundaries of our sociocultural experience, what we're really doing is expanding our literary community. We're inviting influence and embracing the serendipitous power of the unfamiliar. We're banking on the reciprocal nature of the word—that when we give ourselves over to a text, that text gives back. And we're trusting in the notion that being a good citizen starts with getting to know our neighbors.

Participate in the Local Scene

As important as reading is, we can't experience the full value of a literary community until we get out and actually get to know some of our living literary neighbors. In big cities and small towns, we find writers congregating around universities and colleges, community writing groups, libraries, arts organizations, even coffee shops and bookstores. And these writers are just like us—accustomed to the lonely reality of the writing life but also eager for the camaraderie that comes from being part of something larger than ourselves. This is the social contract of every good writing community—to find the support we need, we have to be that support for others.

And it all starts with showing up. I've heard poet John Poch talk about driving all over Atlanta in the early 1990s to attend poetry readings. Back then he was a student "hungry for poetry." "I wanted what these poets had (a life of making poems), and I wanted to meet them, hear their stories, their experiences, and even the sound of their voices and their cadences."[3] With no Internet to streamline his search, Poch looked up events in the newspaper and even called English departments at local universities. Today when his own students can't make it to a reading "because they have yoga or a spin class or they're watching some new Netflix series," Poch just shakes his head. Poets should want poetry, he says, and it's frustrating to see writers pass over so many free, easy opportunities.

Universities typically sponsor regular literary events, but even without a creative writing program nearby, plenty of community-based events are just a Google search away. Check out activity calendars at libraries, arts centers, bookstores, and coffee shops. Follow their social media threads—no newspaper or phone calls required. Then we mark our calendars, grab a friend, and head out hungry for some literature.

It's worth talking a bit more about this idea of hunger. Most Fridays during the school year, my English department hosts a reading series, and while 150 students usually attend, far fewer are actually present. Sure their butts are in chairs, but half of them are on their phones or laptops, playing games, reading email, or scrolling social media. I've seen students watching YouTube and even shopping for clothes while a National Book Award finalist reads from her latest novel. This should go without saying, but good literary citizenship means being hungry enough for literature that we silence our phones, close our laptops, and give the reader or speaker our full attention.

It also means doing a little homework ahead of time: reading something by the author, preparing a question for the Q&A session, bringing some cash to buy a book, and waiting in line to get it signed. And it also means curiosity—not just about the headliner, but about the person sitting in the next seat over or standing behind us in line. Attending local literary events with this kind of curiosity sets us up to discover new writers we admire, find friends and potential collaborators, and cultivate some inspiration for our own work.

Once we begin attending events in our local literary scene, the natural next step is to participate. We might share work with a friend or join a writing group or we may sign up for a time slot at an open-mic night. If we're in a university program or other formal-writing community, there's a good chance that we'll be required to participate in a reading. And that's a good thing. Nothing focuses our revision energy quite like the prospect of reading in public.

Dr. Sarah Jefferis treats public reading as part of her writing process. "I might write a poem, and then I'll memorize eighty percent of it, and then take it up with me to read in public, and I'll suddenly realize that there's a line that's in the wrong place, and I'll move it on the spot." She also appreciates the immediate feedback of a live audience. "Sometimes I'll read something aloud to myself and hate it. But then I'll read it aloud in public and someone will say 'oh, that's really interesting.'"[4] Audience responses help Jefferis remember that her work has a public life of its own and that her own opinion about it is just that—an opinion.

Beyond reading, there are many other ways to get involved. Most literary communities run on volunteer labor, whether it be helping promote an event on social media or showing up early to set up chairs. It might even mean hosting an event or organizing one ourselves if we have the resources. And as usually happens with gestures toward community, we often end up benefiting from the service as much or more than the folks we're helping.

When Melissa Febos was a graduate student in New York City, she and her friends wanted to get to know some of their favorite local writers, but they didn't want to merely write fan letters. They felt they needed "something to offer" when they approached these writers, so they got the idea to start a reading series. "We started with our teachers, and then we began inviting writers that we admired." The reading series was a win–win for everyone. Authors got some exposure, audiences heard some great literature, and Febos and her friends got to know a few of their literary heroes. "A number

READING IN PUBLIC
A CHECKLIST ☑

BEFORE

- ☐ PRACTICE! (WE OWE LISTENERS MORE THAN THE LIVE VERSION OF A BAD AUDIOBOOK)
- ☐ EAT A SNACK
- ☐ DRESS TO MATCH THE VENUE
- ☐ BRING A WATER BOTTLE
- ☐ AND A BREATH MINT
- ☐ PRINT OUT YOUR TEXT (READING OFF A SMARTPHONE IS TACKY)
- ☐ SHOW UP EARLY
- ☐ HIT THE BATHROOM

DURING

- ☐ THANK EVERYONE—THE HOST, THE AUDIENCE, THE ORGANIZATION, YOUR UBER DRIVER!
- ☐ KNOW WHO'S IN THE CROWD (NOT EVERYONE IS READY FOR THAT GRAPHIC SEX SCENE)
- ☐ BREAK THE ICE WITH A PASSAGE FROM YOUR FAVORITE WRITER
- ☐ TAKE A BREATH, SLOW DOWN, LOOK UP!
- ☐ THE 3 B's (BE SHORT, BE SINCERE, BE SEATED)

AFTER

- ☐ THANK EVERYONE (AGAIN)
- ☐ ANSWER QUESTIONS, BUT WATCH THE CLOCK (NEVER GO OVER TIME)
- ☐ DON'T LEAVE WITHOUT GETTING TO KNOW SOMEONE NEW (THE HOST, OTHER READERS, AUDIENCE MEMBERS)
- ☐ GO CELEBRATE! READING IN PUBLIC ISN'T EASY, BUT IT'S WORTH IT)

FIGURE 3 *"Reading in Public".*

of those writers who came and read have ended up blurbing my books later on," explains Febos. "And they're people I've called on for advice."[5]

Supporting the local community is about channeling our love of literature into action, and when done with the right spirit, we end up learning valuable skills, establishing important relationships, and exposing ourselves to all kinds of new opportunities. But there's a final, slightly more abstract benefit that's worth mentioning. Fiction writer Tim Denevi, who has been active in the Washington, DC, literary scene for years, appreciates community involvement for the perspective it offers. Just being among other writers helps Denevi remember that "our successes don't have to happen all at once, and we can enjoy wherever we are in the process." Celebrating and supporting writers, whether they be old or young, new or experienced, "can remind us of where we've come from, where we're at right now, or where we're heading."[6] It can remind us that with art, as with life, everything worthwhile takes time.

Find Community Online

It's hard to overstate the influence that social media platforms have had on the possibilities of building a writing community. Not only have Twitter, Instagram, and Facebook made the Neil Gaimans and Zadie Smiths of the world more accessible than ever, but they've also put us within reach of thousands of work-a-day writers toiling away largely outside the popular media spotlight. It has never been easier to collaborate, share opinions, or promote our work. And precisely because the Internet has made the writing community so intimate and accessible, it has never been more important that we practice generosity and compassion in our online professional relationships. That the opinions we share are thoughtful, well-informed, and judicious and that we temper our desire for self-promotion with a heavy dose of humility. Consider the following three exemplary citizens—writers who have used social media to share valuable information, support artists they admire, create opportunities for others, and inspire those around them, all while avoiding the taint of shameless self-promotion.

Twitter: @vickjulie

Let's start with Julie Vick, a humor writer in Denver, Colorado, who has more than 8,000 followers on Twitter. Examining a random month of her tweets—say, September 2020—reveals six retweeted submission calls, seven posts celebrating the work of other writers, and seven conversational posts about the writing life. Then there are observations about parenting, remote-work, and pandemic life (it was 2020, after all) and only one personal (albeit funny) overshare about going to the dermatologist for what she thought was a mole but was actually something called a "barnacle of life." And, notably, in all those tweets only once did she post something directly about her own work. The rest of her tweets were all focused on other people.

"For me, Twitter has been a great way to connect with others in the literary community," says Vick. "These relationships have sometimes turned into meeting in person at conferences, finding partners for feedback and co-writing, or other opportunities." Twitter helps Vick feel less isolated as a writer, and as she prepared for the release of her first book, her online community helped answer all kinds of questions. "Social media can have its downsides," she admits. "But one of the big upsides for me has been finding a supportive writing community that has helped demystify a lot of the publishing process."[7]

Facebook and Blogging: Dinty W. Moore

Back in 2010, *Brevity Magazine* founder Dinty W. Moore created a Facebook account but had no idea what he'd use it for. "I posted jokes, updates from airports, and musings on politics and popular culture," he remembers, but it was a few quotes on the writing life that got the most attention. He eventually decided to make sharing quotes a daily practice, and in a little over a decade he has shared upwards of 2,800 posts, each garnering dozens, sometimes hundreds of responses from online friends. His posts were so popular that they drew the attention of an editor who messaged Moore on Facebook about putting together a manuscript—what would eventually become a successful little volume of writing advice called *The Mindful Writer.*

"Most of my writing life has been spent in small college towns containing just a tiny cadre of literary writers," says Moore. "Social media has been perfect for extending my range of contacts and feeling a deeper sense of community."[8] Watching Moore over the years though, it is obvious that he cares as much about creating community for others as finding it for himself. In addition to his work on Facebook, Moore's literary journal *Brevity* and its associated blog have become an important online hub for all things creative nonfiction. *Brevity Blog* receives tens of thousands of visits each month and hosts content produced by a wide range of writers who share book reviews, submission calls, craft discussions and interviews not for pay but for the chance to help out another writer.

Instagram: @morgan__gayle

As an English major at the University of Mary Washington and then as a graduate student at American University in Saint Louis, Morgan Harding felt frustrated that her courses included so few books by Black authors (and Black women in particular). Now, as an independent bookseller, she uses her influence to promote underrepresented voices all over the place. In addition to a stint reviewing books on YouTube, she has since 2018, hosted a monthly reading group called "A Seat at the Table," sponsored by the Politics & Prose bookstore in Washington, DC. Harding describes the group "as a space for all Black women [to be] heard, seen, and celebrated."[9]

She's also on Instagram as "Paperback Morgan," making regular posts about books for her almost 2,000 followers. Her Instagram account includes book covers, self-portraits, the occasional video, and artfully posed still-lifes of books called "flatlays." Along with these images, she offers carefully crafted micro-book reviews written in a casual, conversational tone that reveal both her personality and her long experience with close reading. Frank and funny, Harding uses her Instagram presence to elevate writers she admires, and while she's not the flashiest or most popular bookstagrammer out there, her posts feel utterly authentic and completely committed to supporting her community.

Social media has made it easier than ever to build a writing community, but just a few minutes on any one of these platforms is sometimes a depressing lesson in the dark side of human nature. Why, we might ask, do social media feeds, comment threads, and online reviews so often devolve into partisan flag-waving, name calling, and virtue signaling at the expense of just about everyone? The problem, according to technologist Jaron Lanier, is not in algorithms but in our brains: "Negative emotions such as fear and anger well up more easily and dwell in us longer than positive emotions."[10] When we're online, our own human nature tends to amplify, encourage, and reward controversial, combative, flippant, dismissive, antagonistic content—and all that noise can make community next to impossible.

Online literary citizenship means resisting this pull toward the negative. That's not to say there's no place for criticism on the Internet, but if we have something negative to say about a writer or their work, we probably ought to ask ourselves, is it constructive, or is it simply mean? Is it a fair representation of the author's work or are we cherry-picking individual lines out of context? Does it contribute to the critical understanding of an author's work, or does it simply make us look clever?

This is standard "golden rule" stuff, but given the amount of vitriol on the Internet, it needs to be said. Especially since the Internet makes contacting authors so easy. Before social media, authors could pretty easily avoid negative criticism if they wanted to. But today everyone is just an @ sign away. Carmen Maria Machado, who has tweeted about the frustration of seeing readers tag authors in negative reviews, compares this in-your-face online criticism to "ripping out a bad review that you had written in the newspaper and then mailing it to the home of the author."[11] That would be some next-level pettiness, but on social media this kind of confrontation happens all too often. Perhaps the most basic principle is this—if we feel that sharing something negative will actually contribute to the literary conversation, then go ahead and post it—but for heaven's sake, don't tag the author.

And if there's anything more pathetic than a social media feed full of petty shots at strangers, it might just be an endless feed of shameless self-promotion. Consider the three examples from earlier: Vick, Moore, and Harding have made a space for themselves on social media, but they've done that not by talking incessantly about their own achievements but by offering something of value to the community. Whether these authors post a Twitter thread of distracting wit, daily quotes of literary inspiration, or offer a regular feed of thoughtful book reviews, each has put in the work to make the community better. And that, hands down, is the best promotional tool of all.

Share Your (Informed) Opinion

Offering one's opinion has become a twenty-first-century way of life, and that extends well beyond the realm of social media. Angie wants me to recommend a plumber. Glassdoor wants me to rate my job. Yelp wants to know if I enjoyed my dinner, and Uber wants a report on the drive home. And that doesn't even include Amazon—they want my opinion on everything, from saucepans and soccer balls to wallets and weedkiller. But they also want me to rate every book I've ever ordered.

Is there anything wrong with a site that asks us to rate our kitchenware and gardening supplies in the same breath that we rate Maya Angelou and Joan Didion? Book critic Laura Miller appreciates informal online book reviews because they show us "the infinite variety of ways that a person can experience a book," which is a rather euphemistic take on a genre that can range from cloying praise to bitter diatribe. But her point is worth reflecting on. "Each review represents an instance of someone taking a chance," writes Miller. "Opening the covers of a book and allowing an author's words into her head with the hope that something magical might result."[12]

But when a book fails to produce the "magic" that we're hoping for, it can be tempting to act as if we've somehow been duped into reading it. Or worse, as if the book were merely a consumer product—an uncomfortable pair of Converse or a faulty alarm clock. A book is (at least attempting to be) a work of art, and passing judgment on a book the same way we pass judgment on footwear or home electronics diminishes both the role of literature and our roles as readers.

Consuming art, according to Lewis Hyde, is different from consuming stuff. "Even if we have paid a fee at the door of the museum or concert hall [or used a debit card on Amazon.com], when we are touched by a work of art something comes to us which has nothing to do with the price."[13] Purchase a pair of shoes and we have every right to expect them to hold together. Purchase entrance to an art museum and the only thing we have a "right" to is a polite stroll through the gallery. The museum makes no guarantee that we will enjoy ourselves. There's no promise that the art will be easy to understand, that the artist will share our aesthetic or political leanings, or even that we will be the target audience for any of the work in the museum. To critique an art exhibit, we need not only some clarity about our personal aesthetic but also an understanding of art history, of sociocultural context and of the larger artistic conversation certain artists are engaged in.

Whether we're typing online reviews, writing longform book reviews for traditional publications, posting flatlays for our bookstagram followers or recording video reviews for YouTube or TikTok, Hyde's museum metaphor can be useful. After all, when we buy a book we're not merely purchasing paper and ink, binding and cover art. We're purchasing entrance to an author's world, and if we have any hope of obtaining the priceless "something" that Hyde promises from art, if we want to serve as a guide to others who might consider making the same journey, then we have certain obligations to text, author, and reader.

First, read the whole book. Sure, I've stopped reading plenty of books before finishing the first chapter. But reviewing a book I haven't finished would be like taking a glance at the first painting I see on a museum wall, deciding I don't like it, and then walking out and telling everyone else in line that they're wasting their money. A book is an experience, and I have no obligation to finish it, but if I'm going to pass judgment on it for others then it is unethical to base my judgment solely on its first moments.

Second, approach each book on its own terms. As Janet Hulstrand explains, responsible reviewers make judgments "on the basis of what kind of book the author intended to write, not on the basis of what kind of book the reader expected to read, or wished to read."[14] If I went to a gallery exhibit of contemporary street art, I couldn't rightly complain about the absence of Renaissance portraits. If I'm reviewing a murder mystery, it would be unfair to compare it to *Pride & Prejudice*. Books are written in conversation with other books—a conversation that involves genre, subject matter, structure, sociocultural context, aesthetics, and even marketing. So when we set out to write a review, we ought to at least be aware of the conversation we're joining.

Third, write in service of the potential reader. Huff Post's Neal Wooten reminds us, "Reviews are about books and for readers; they're not about you."[15] That's not to say our opinion doesn't matter. Only that we ought to back it up. Better than a review such as "I just couldn't get into it" might be a review that says, "The author dwells for maybe too long on backstory in the first few chapters." Better than "I got so bored" might be "Readers who prefer a fast-paced narrative may struggle." To return to the museum analogy, consider that line of people queued up outside the exhibit, waiting to go in. What might be helpful for them to know? If as

I leave the museum I holler at the crowd "I hated it!" or "The first room is so boring!" that doesn't give them much to go on, but it does tell them quite a bit about me.

Fourth, recognize the harm of bad-faith reviews: For a well-known book with tens of thousands of reviews, a hastily written, overly harsh, or uninformed review will likely get lost in the noise, but when it comes to lesser-known books, negative reviews can be devastating. Practicing good literary citizenship means that our opinions, positive or negative, be couched in thoughtful, informed, and respectful language.

To Wooten, such critical conscientiousness means easing off the one-star trigger finger. "If a book is well-written and well-edited, it should never get less than a three-star review." *Never* is a hardline position, but let's hear him out. "Stories are subjective, and just because it didn't appeal to you doesn't mean it won't appeal to someone else." Wooten believes, and I tend to agree, that one-star reviews should be reserved for books with "no redeeming qualities whatsoever." And lest we accuse Wooten of being too soft, he's just as picky with his positive reviews. "A five-star review should be for a book that has everything: good writing, good editing, and a story that makes you want to read it again and tell your friends about." If we're too free with five-star reviews, it cheapens the rating. Not all good books are great books, and it's okay to be honest about that too.

In the end, leaving even a half-way thoughtful critique on a website doesn't require much effort, but if we find ourselves truly engaged by a book, perhaps it's time to consider producing a more in-depth review, maybe for a traditional publication such as a newspaper, magazine, or literary journal, or even for a new-media platform such as YouTube, Instagram, TikTok, and others. These reviews contribute not merely to a marketing data set but to an ongoing community discussion, and they demand more knowledge of the context in which the book was written.

If an informal online review leans heavily on reader response, then more formal reviews tend to engage the other critical modes: new critical attention to form, an emphasis on aesthetics and language, and historical, cultural, or socioeconomic contexts as well. Whatever the critical lens we rely on, our formal book review should cue into the ways a book is engaging with the broader world and should provide readers not merely a glimpse of what the book has to offer, but a suggestion of why it might be important to read.

Another reason to write formal book reviews is for the experience. Editors at many journals, newspapers, magazines, and websites are looking for well-written, thoughtful reviews that help readers sift through the thousands of books that are published each year. Pitching and writing such reviews can help us get to know editors, provide valuable experience writing for an actual publication, and give us some practice contributing in a public way to the literary community (for more information on publishing book reviews, visit joeyfranklin.com/writershustle).

TRYING TO FIND our place in a community can feel daunting. It requires reading more broadly than we're probably inclined to. It requires getting out and meeting people, participating in local events, and maybe even helping out. It requires finding ways to support our fellow writers while taking ourselves seriously as professionals. For some it can all feel too calculating, too much like "careerism." Maybe we resent the unavoidable reality that who we know often matters more than it should. Maybe we don't like the jarring sounds of words like *networking* or *professionalism* alongside words like *inspiration* and *art*.

And yet few of us will muster the time or resources necessary for inspiration or art if we don't seek out the support of our fellow writers. "A huge part of professionalization in writing is just building habits and designing a lifestyle that can support your creative work,"[16] says Melissa Febos. Citizenship, in the end, is about developing relationships that support that lifestyle. The writing must happen, and no amount of literary socializing will make up for time at the keyboard. But as Febos says, "what some people think of as the 'pure' parts of being a writer can't happen if the other things aren't in place." And for that, there are few things more helpful than a community we can trust.

4.

EARNING A MENTOR

During my senior year of college, I quite unexpectedly won first prize in a national essay contest, which meant an embarrassingly gratuitous cash prize and the publication of my essay in a Random House anthology of young essayists. Pretty heady stuff for a twenty-five-year-old still uncertain about being a writer. I enjoyed a brief moment in the campus spotlight: pats on the back from fellow students, handshakes from plenty of faculty, and even a brief interview with our alumni magazine. The essay itself helped me get into graduate school, and maybe gave me a false notion of what it took to get published, but the most lasting lessons from the whole experience came from conversations with two of my writing professors.

The first lesson occurred in Patrick Madden's office at about the same time as the alumni magazine was scheduling my photo-op for the interview. I was riding pretty high, and Madden congratulated me on both the publication and the cash. But then he said, "Don't get used to it." We laughed, but then he went on, with just a hint of an edge in his voice. "Seriously," he said. "It's all downhill from here. You probably won't make money like that on another publication for the rest of your life." Madden's point? Don't get a big head. Most of the time, being a writer means lots of work without much recognition or money to show for it.

The second lesson came a short time later, when I bumped into Doug Thayer, the formidable seventy-seven-year-old patriarch of the creative writing faculty who had attended the Iowa Writer's Workshop in the 1950s and then spent the next sixty years putting the fear of God into students who were often long on literary dreams but short on the necessary work ethic. "I heard you got some sort of publication." He said to me in the hallway of the English building. He allowed me to recount the story that I'd become fond of telling, and when I finished he held the silence between us just a little longer than I would have liked. "Well . . . Don't let it be a flash in the pan," he finally said. And then he walked away.

Thayer's lesson? Basically, the same as Madden's. If I wanted to make a career out of writing, it was going to take a lot more than one published essay and one surprising paycheck. What I heard? Keep your head down, go write your fingers raw, and then come back and talk to me in a decade.

And they were both right. That essay may have paved my way to graduate school, and the money certainly helped, but it took three years and dozens more submissions to publish another piece, and all my subsequent writing paydays have been much more modest, if they've offered anything at all. What's still paying dividends, though? Two humbling lessons from important mentors in my early writing life.

Do I Really Need Help?

For some, the word *mentor* might conjure old-fashioned, patriarchal, elitist notions of faux meritocracy. Or it might smack of careerism and the kind of schmoozing one imagines going on in the halls of a business school. Mentoring relationships at their worst can preserve highly problematic power imbalances that perpetuate structures of privilege and prejudice in any professional environment. But at their best, mentoring relationships represent the ultimate promise of a supportive writing community, the highest form of literary citizenship.

As we've already discussed in Chapter 3, every writer needs a support system: a friend, a roommate, a spouse, a parent, a curious barista. Someone to read drafts and say, "you're doing great;" someone to watch the kids on a deadline day; someone who will listen to us vent about rejections; someone to refill the tea. But writers eventually need more than a cheerleading squad. More than an open-mic night. More than friends who can swap reading suggestions. We need the guidance of seasoned experts who will slash our self-indulgent sentences. We need confidantes who can help us turn the debilitating pain of rejection into motivation to keep working. We need consultants who know their way around publication agreements, job offers, and contracts. Writing is a craft and a trade, but also an art and a business. And as with most aesthetic and professional endeavors, it helps to have a mentor who can model not only ways of working but also ways of living.

What can a mentor really do for us? Consider a few examples:

Mentor as Honest Reader

Among the more famous mentor readers was Ezra Pound, who reviewed early drafts by Robert Frost, Earnest Hemingway, and, most notably, T. S. Eliot. In an act of enthusiastic editing that has proved as much a gift to English majors as to the larger literary world, Pound convinced Eliot to cut "a great deal of superfluous matter"[1] from early drafts of his epic poem "The Wasteland." Pound referred to his effort as a "Caesarean operation,"[2] and Eliot himself admitted that the poem "owes more to Pound's surgery than anyone can realise."[3]

Mentor as Bar Raiser

For novelist Janet Fitch, it was tough-talking LA novelist Kate Braverman. "What she cared about most was the emotional and lyric power of language," Fitch tells me. In workshop, it was Braverman's duty to "defend literature against your lousy writing." She could be cruel, admits Fitch. "But when you delivered something really beautiful, her praise was heavenly. You never doubted how you were doing."[4]

Mentor as Intellectual Guide

Essayist José Orduña met David Lazar, his first writing mentor, while studying film and video at Columbia College in Chicago. "By chance I took a nonfiction writing workshop [from Lazar], and immediately, I realized, this is the kind of work I want to do." Orduña went on to take more classes with Lazar, and each course expanded his literary awareness. "The most important thing David did was introduce me to a literary tradition that I didn't know existed," says Orduña. But Lazar's work as a mentor went beyond the classroom. As Orduña neared the end of his schooling, Lazar encouraged him to consider MFA programs, stayed in touch with him after he left Chicago, offered advice on various graduate schools, and wrote letters of recommendation. "He has been a champion of my work and a good friend," says Orduña. "Having David in my corner has always made me feel like I have an intellectual home that I don't think I would have if I hadn't met him."[5]

Mentor as Voice-Whisperer

Novelist Alexander Chee studied under Annie Dillard at Wesleyan University, and he credits Dillard with helping coax out his voice. "You could think that your voice as a writer would just emerge naturally, all on its own, but you're wrong . . . The voice is in fact trapped, nervous, lazy," writes

Chee. Dillard left copious notes in the margins of Chee's drafts, including this zinger: "Sometimes you write amazing sentences, and sometimes it's amazing you can write a sentence." But she also helped him identify and focus on expanding his best work, and she helped him cultivate faith in himself. "You are the only one of you," Dillard reportedly told him. "Your unique perspective, at this time, in our age, whether it's on Tunis or the trees outside your window, is what matters."[6]

Mentor as Interventionist

Novelist Rick Moody's shortlist of mentors includes Angela Carter, who spent two semesters at Brown University where Moody was a student. Carter showed Moody "how to live a little bit, and how to act like a writer, instead of merely dreaming of being one." In Carter's presence, Moody "felt not only that [he] grew as a writer but that [he] improved as a person."[7] Carter had a "willingness to intervene personally"[8] in his education and, he says, "the audacity to tell me that drugs were not good for my work and that I was reading crap."[9]

Mentor as Firm Hand

Poet Tracy K. Smith recalls two professors who reviewed her MFA thesis. She says that one reviewer, "a respected poet and critic (and, as it happens, a man), demolished my poems, leveling my project as a whole with comments like 'these poems fall prey to the snare of infantile narcissism.'" In contrast, another reviewer, Lucie Brock-Broido, offered "measured praise and thoughtful reflections," that felt to Smith "like a firm hand at the center of my back, assuring me of its comforting presence while pushing gently forward." Comparing these two approaches, Smith admits that both assessments were probably accurate, "but while one succeeded in silencing me for months," the other "managed to dangle the promise of meaning and music just near enough and just far enough away to make me want—no, need—to keep striving for it."[10]

Mentor as Permission Granter

Novelist Alissa Nutting credits Kate Bernheimer for giving her confidence in her own eccentricities. After spending a year in her MFA program writing what Nutting describes as "really, really bad"[11] realist fiction, she entered Bernheimer's workshop determined to "clean the freak right out" of her fiction. Instead, Nutting wrote a story that "involved werewolves and a boy who sat on chocolate bars nude to melt them with his body heat." Nutting expected Bernheimer's feedback to focus on how to make her story "less strange," but instead Bernheimer said, "Whatever you're doing, don't stop." This was the mentorship Nutting needed—permission to be herself, to follow her own instincts. "What a relief it was to see how I could focus on my obsessions instead of bury them."[12]

Mentor as Juggling Expert

Poet Kathy Lou Schultz met Myung Mi Kim while Schultz was a student at San Francisco State University. "From the time I nervously entered [Kim's] classroom, I was struck by her articulate passion. She talked about writing in a way that my previous teachers never had."[13] Kim pushed Schultz to think more critically about feminism, politics, and poetics, but she also taught her about balance. "In Myung I also saw for the first time what it might mean to live one's life as a poet. I watched Myung juggle teaching, motherhood, marriage, and her own strong creative drives. I watched her carve out a space for her work when writing is not a choice but a necessity."[14]

How to Find a Mentor

The mentors in these examples offered writers what they needed at the right moment, even if the writers didn't know they needed it: advice, critique, motivation, a model. Mentors help us see our strengths and weaknesses. They help us open doors and sometimes show us ones we didn't know existed. They help give us permission to be ourselves on the page, but they also instill the courage to believe that we don't need anyone's permission at all.

And while many of these examples come from academic settings, a mentoring relationship doesn't have to start as a student/teacher relationship. In fact, merely being a student in a certain class will not turn that professor into a mentor. These sorts of professional connections are best developed naturally over time as we devote ourselves to the writing life and demonstrate commitment to the writing community. For writers in school this means not just attending class but also guest lectures, poetry nights, and Q&A sessions with visiting authors. And for writers outside of school it may mean signing up for a workshop at the local civic center, or looking out for writers we admire at open-mic nights at the local coffee shop. It means setting writing goals, working toward them, and then seeking out writers who might have some good advice on how to do it all more effectively.

So how do we approach potential mentors, though, without imposing on the busy schedules of overworked and underpaid writers? How do we ask for a relationship without forcing one? If we're already participating in our writing community, chances are an opportunity will arise organically as part of that work, as it did for Alissa Nutting, Tracy K. Smith, and others I've mentioned. But more than likely, finding a mentor will require a little bit of hustle.

Be Bold, but Do the Work

A favorite example from history is Emily Dickinson, who by age 35 had written more than 1,000 poems but had shared only a small portion of them with family and friends. Recognizing her need for a "preceptor" (or teacher), Dickinson penned a letter to Thomas Wentworth Higginson, who wrote for *The Atlantic Monthly* and had in 1862 published some notes of advice and encouragement to would-be writers that he titled "Letter to a Young Contributor." In her reply to Higginson's open letter, Dickinson included four original poems and a short note that began simply and directly: "MR. HIGGINSON,—Are you too deeply occupied to say if my verse is alive?."[15]

Dickinson's actions offer here two lessons on reaching out to potential mentors. First, be bold. Mr. Higginson was undoubtedly busy. In his lifetime, he wrote 500 essays and thirty-five books. Even if Dickinson had an inkling that her work was any good, she showed guts in sending that letter. The second, more important lesson is this: do the work. Dickinson did not send her letter after writing one poem or ten poems but hundreds of poems. She may not have been submitting her work all over the place or reading it to audiences in some Boston lyceum, but through poem after poem she was transforming herself into a writer. That serious investment in herself as a poet most certainly gave her the confidence to contact Higginson in the first place. And in the end, it was not the pluck of her letter alone that earned her a mentor. Higginson recognized Dickinson as a "wholly new and original poetic genius."[16] Not that we all have to be "wholly new and original," but we certainly ought to put in our own serious effort before asking another writer for help.

Aim for Authenticity

Reaching out is an important first step in developing professional relationships, and a little boldness can go a long way, especially if we've done the work to earn it. But if we treat our professional relationships as business arrangements, we may end up alienating people. As a graduate student, writer E. J. Levy made friends with a well-known author who visited her campus. Levy knew the relationship could be helpful to her career, but she wasn't sure how to maintain it. Someone suggested she "cultivate the contact by sending an e-mail every six months or so." Ultimately, says Levy, "that advice was ruinous." Her calculated efforts "turned a sincere

FIGURE 4 *"The Emily Dickinson Guide to Finding a Mentor,"* All quotes taken from *Thomas Wentworth Higginson, "Emily Dickinson's Letters,"* The Atlantic Monthly, *October 1891, https://www.theatlantic.com/magazine/archive/1891/10/emily-dickinsons-letters/306524.*

and admiring bond into a creepy contact, merely instrumental." Instead of "cultivating a contact," Levy suggests we "follow up only when it's actually important to do so"—when we need advice, a blurb, or some other help. "Otherwise I want my exchanges to be free of the taint of such professional considerations, to be honest engagement, one writer to another."[17]

Respect Boundaries

One summer, the novelist Spencer Hyde agreed to help a promising young student with his graduate school application but slowly came to regret it. "I started out in May helping him with his personal statement and a writing sample," says Hyde. "Then he asked if he could send another story, and another, and I read that too." Hyde agreed to keep reading partly because the student's work had impressed him but also because Hyde is a nice guy. By mid-summer though, after meeting nearly every Friday and sometimes reading two stories a week, it became clear that this student would take as much as Hyde was willing to give. The last straw came one week in July when the student, who'd already emailed Hyde two stories, sent a third with a note that said, "Hey, I'm working on this piece to send to a journal. Could you look at it also?"

Reluctantly, Hyde agreed, and they met that Friday to discuss the three stories. But the following Monday when the student sent another batch of stories, Hyde just ignored them. "This has been a learning experience for me too," says Hyde. "It's hard to say no to a writer with such talent, but I definitely started feeling taken advantage of."[18] They eventually talked about the situation, and because Hyde really is a nice guy, they kept meeting but only every month or so. And this is the real detail to remember. The kindness of our mentors is likely what will draw us to them. They're usually the type of people who want to help. But it's on us to make sure we don't exploit their good will.

Consider Identity-Based Support

I've been teaching literature and creative writing for more than a decade. I've published a couple of books, I present at conferences, and I coedit a twenty-year-old literary magazine. I like to think I've got enough experience to help any new writer who knocks on my door, but I am also a white, heterosexual, cisgender male whose cultural experience may limit my value as a resource for some writers. Living and writing as a member of a traditionally underrepresented or marginalized group brings with it unique challenges, and for many successful writers, finding identity-based mentorship has been not only helpful but essential.

Poet Neil Aitken, who is of Chinese and Scottish descent, appreciates his mentors of color for contributing "a wealth of insights into not just cultural and familial patterns and concerns, but also to the very isolating experience of being alone in a predominantly white space (be it the classroom, the reading event, the academy, or the realm of publishing)." Aitken first found identity-based mentorship in his graduate program at UC Riverside working under Chris Abani, Juan Felipe Herrera, and Michael Jayme: "There is something amazing about sitting down with a mentor who shares your face, whose life in some way or another, has paralleled your own, whose journey through this world is marked with common struggles, common injustices, and common sorrows."[19]

And for Aitken, more important than individual mentorship has been "the experience of being immersed in a community of writers of color"[20] through organizations such as Kundiman, a New York-based nonprofit "dedicated to nurturing generations of writers and readers of Asian American Literature."[21] As an attendee at Kundiman's annual writing retreat, Aitken was introduced to an Asian American poetic tradition "far more vast in its scope and diverse in its experiences"[22] than what he'd read in college.

Before attending his first retreat, Aitken says he harbored the erroneous notion that "as a mixed race Chinese-Scottish Canadian," he might not belong in the Asian American literary community. Being at the retreat helped him realize that "whatever anxieties I harbored going in, were not mine alone—and that instead, we all had similar fears, similar worries about how we fit or did not fit with the idea of 'Asian American.'" As Aitken sees it, participating in community experiences such as Kundiman "offer[s] you a family you didn't know existed, that you never knew you needed—and as a family, Kundiman becomes a life-changing and life-long relationship."[23]

Organizations such as Kundiman are at work all across the country providing nurturing spaces of affirmation, support, and mentoring for a wide variety of communities. Along with Kundiman, some of the more well-known organizations include:

- Cave Canem (cavecanempoets.org: "Committed to cultivating the artistic and professional growth of African American poets")

- Canto Mundo (Cantomundo.org: "A national poetry organization that cultivates a community of Latinx poets through workshops, symposia, and public readings")

- Disability Visibility Project (disabilityarts.online: "An online community dedicated to creating, sharing, and amplifying disability media and culture")

- International Women's Writing Guild (iww.org: "A place where all women writers feel welcome, inspired, and empowered by skills, resources, and mentoring")

- Lambda Literary (lambadaliterary.org: "A space where LGBTQ voices are centered, not sidelined—honored, not denigrated")

- Macondo (macandowriters.com: "An association of socially-engaged writers . . . from all genres who work on geographic, cultural, economic, gender, and spiritual borders")

- The Radius of Arab American writers (arabamericanwriters.org: "A national organization that provides mentoring, community, and support for Arab American writers and those with roots in the Arabic speaking world and the diaspora")

- Voices of Our Nation (vonavoices.org: "A community-based organization that puts writers of color, their narratives, voices, and experiences at the center of all conversations")

Many other organizations work at the local and regional level and on college campuses around the country. In addition, many writers find identity-based support through informal community gatherings. Poet Daphne Gottlieb describes discovering just such a community at a local poetry reading in San Francisco. Gottlieb grew up writing poetry, but as she became an adult the practical needs of life led her to an editing job rather than something in creative writing. "But then . . . a friend brought me to a reading. And, as the cliche goes, it changed my life."[24] In this group of "pierced, tattooed, shaved, hairy, leftist, ultracaffeinated" poets, Gottlieb found inspiration. "Seeing all the young writers get up, shout bile, and purr glitter with all of their hearts made me shriek inside—*I used to do that! I CAN do that!*" She started writing, and "thanks to invitations from around the community," she started reading in public. She made friends with whom she held "writing dates . . . sitting in cafés and scrawling." She gave more readings, met more people, and eventually she "was invited to join a group of queer female writers." She began organizing her own events, met local editors and publishers, and established herself as a fixture in her local LGBTQ writing community. "I have never taken a step forward without sideways glances toward them. These female poets showed me how they made their chapbooks, explained how they got into certain reading series, shared calls for submissions, and helped me book tours."

Gottlieb's story may sound remarkable, but it represents what we can accomplish when we find the right community for our work. And it underscores the mentoring role of the community itself. Even if we lack direct access to a traditional mentor, we can find encouragement, council, and critique from the writers all around us.

Don't Underestimate the Books on Your Shelf

For all this talk about soliciting mentors and finding the right community support, it's important to remember that for many writers, the first and best mentors have been books themselves. And not just as examples of how to write but as voices of permission as well. Aimee Nezhukumatathil's textual mentor has been Naomi Shihab Nye: "Her poems are comfort food for me, a place and a space where I feel both independent and at home, reassured by the company of a writer's voice that clicks and laughs in syncopation with my own." She finds herself in Nye's books—"My hunger for family, my hunger for wanting to share overlooked quiet moments—here in the folded pages of her collections, I am sated."[25]

Balance Expectations

Part of the value of working with mentors is the chance to scrutinize the experience of professionals we admire. They offer front-row seats to their writing process, their teaching style, their strategies for publication, their conduct at public events, and even the state of their private lives. Such proximity may increase our admiration and gratitude for our mentors, but it will also undoubtedly remind us that for all their professional success, they are in the end human, just like us. On the one hand, that reminder can be reassuring (for instance, every time I find myself pulled in different directions by work and family life, I remember that my mentor Patrick Madden is doing the same thing, but he's got twice as many kids as I do). On the other hand, bearing witness to the frailties and failures of those we look up to can be disheartening.

And yet the human aspect of a mentoring relationship is unavoidable, which is why some writers find the notion of mentoring so problematic. Take poet Paisley Rekdal, for instance, who came up as a writer without much in the way of real mentorship. She had plenty of opportunities, but, she explains, she "never trusted anyone enough."[26] She admits that early in her career, she was sometimes "ruthless in [her] rejection of potential mentors," passing over help because "one was too lazy" or "too grasping." Maybe "this one competed with her [own] students," and "that one got high before class." She passed on one mentor who seemed too young and inexperienced and another whose timid personality felt like "a feminist betrayal." She recognizes now that in her "search for the perfect mentor, I overlooked a number of people who certainly would have been good enough."

But Rekdal's resistance to mentoring came at least partially out of self-preservation. She lost faith in some would-be mentors when overhearing their casual racism ("so-and-so got his job or prize due to affirmative action"), and she lost faith in others—particularly men—who often "carried with them the faint whiff of sexual attraction, sometimes even predation."[27] And while she makes no apologies for distancing herself from racists and creepy men, looking back, Rekdal believes she may have been "too fastidious—or just naive—about certain emotional entanglements of mentorship." On the one hand, Rekdal can see that "the personal traits and failings—the person—of the mentor doesn't matter so much as the information this mentor has to offer." But on the other hand, she says "the mentor as person is all that matters." To Rekdal, "mentorship at its heart may be practical, but it is also messy." And because she could not find a mentor who fulfilled both her personal and professional expectations, she chose to go it alone.

Of course, *going it alone* isn't always about rejecting every mentor that comes our way. Sometimes it means recognizing when a mentorship has run its course. As poet Tony Hoagland developed as a writer, he discovered that even in the case of his most "influential teacher[s] . . . it became at some point necessary for me to reject them, to step outside the perimeter of their approval or disapproval."[28] As differences in aesthetic or professional priorities emerged, Hoagland recognized the need to go in his own direction.

And now as a professor and mentor himself, Hoagland sees his own students doing the same to him. "At such times, I am sorry to report that my feelings are wounded," writes Hoagland. But he tries to remember that they are simply "trying to move to deep water, where they can swim for themselves."[29]

As Hoagland suggests, to negotiate an ongoing mentor relationship is to "negotiate the contradictory needs of being nourished and being independent."[30] And while not every mentor relationship will end in this kind of rejection, we do well to remember that the goal of such a relationship is to help the novice writer find their own feet and that each of us will eventually want, and no doubt need to stand on our own.

ATTENDING A CONFERENCE, RETREAT, OR RESIDENCY

One spring night in Los Angeles, Patrick Madden and I attended the live-audience taping of a radio interview between John D'Agata, author of the series *A New History of the Essay*, and Michael Silverblatt, host of the KCRW radio program *Bookworm*. The event, held in conjunction with the Association of Writers and Writing Programs (AWP) conference, drew about 100 people to a small art space in a warehouse district a few miles from the convention center. I remember joking with Pat and others in the audience about how difficult it had been to find the building, how there had been no signs, no address numbers, and few streetlights; how my Uber driver had noted the lack of windows on the building and the solitary door with no handle and said, "Are you sure this is the right spot?" Everyone in the audience, it seemed, had groped around the exterior of the building until they'd finally found the poorly marked entrance around back.

We all eventually settled in for what would have been a pleasant but unremarkable half-hour discussion on the history of the essay if not for what happened about ten minutes into the recording session. D'Agata and Silverblatt were sitting on a stage at one end of the hall in the middle of their conversation when several loud knocks filled the room. Silverblatt paused the interview and we all listened. Someone was outside, as lost as everyone else had been, and was now trying to enter the building through that door with no handle, the door which, incidentally, was located almost center stage, exactly between D'Agata and Silverblatt. Not knowing what else to do, a staff member opened the door, and a bespectacled man stepped into the room, blinking. He looked at D'Agata and Silverblatt in their chairs and then out at the audience, and said, "Oh shit." Then, as everyone chuckled, he scurried out of the spotlight, and the interview continued.

A half hour later, Pat and I stood outside on the curb waiting for an Uber when the same bespectacled man emerged from the building. I said something stupid like "That was quite the entrance," and we shared a nervous laugh. I offered him a seat in our Uber back to the conference center, and on the drive I learned that his name was Dan, that he was an essayist like me, and that he taught at a university in Kansas City. We all ended up going to dinner together, spent the evening talking about teaching, writing, and research, and when we parted ways at the end of the night, I didn't think I'd see him again. But we bumped into each other at the next AWP in Washington, DC, and caught up over dinner. This time we exchanged emails, and just like that our writerly friendship was born. Dan and I have since crossed paths at nearly every AWP conference, and I'm always happy to hear what he's up to and read what he's working on. And he's been a good friend and a conscientious reader of my own work.

I share this story because it highlights the difficult-to-quantify value of public gatherings like writing conferences, retreats, and residencies. Sure there's the chance to learn from panel discussions, workshops, lectures, and book exhibits, not to mention the formal opportunities to meet other professionals—but often the most valuable moments are the ones we can't plan for.

Of course, because there are so many different events, and because each event is tailored to writers at different stages of development (and because words like *conference*, *retreat*, *residency*, and *workshop* are sometimes used interchangeably), it can be hard to know which events might be right for us. So first let's define each type of event, and then we'll discuss how to choose between them.

Defining Terms

The writing conference: Usually held over a long weekend, these gatherings attract hundreds, sometimes thousands of writers to a convention center, hotel conference space, or university campus. Attendees can apply to present their own work or simply participate as audience members at panel discussions, lectures, breakout sessions, and readings on various artistic and practical aspects of the writing life.

Some conferences, such as the annual AWP conference I mentioned earlier, cast a wide net, topically and otherwise. In any given hour during the AWP conference (which attracts 13,000+ attendees each year), there might be a session on character development in LGBTQ fiction, historical research in spiritual memoirs, or tips for teaching poetry in prisons. Other conferences cater to a narrower crowd. There are conferences for sci-fi writers, for journalists, for personal essayists, and for romance writers. There are conferences at the local, regional, national, and even international level. And though conferences can feel like passive events with lots of sitting and listening, for a writer with hustle they can offer a firehose blast of inspiration and an almost incessant opportunity to meet other writing professionals.

The writing retreat: Think summer camp for writers without all the lake swimming or fireside singalongs (though not always without firesides). Writing retreats can be as short as a weekend stay at a cabin or bed and breakfast or as long as several weeks in a university dorm or artist colony, and they're built on intimate interaction: writing workshops, one-on-one mentoring, public readings, private writing time, and even planned social activities. There are retreats for poets, for memoirists, and for novelists. For YA writers and romance writers. There are retreats for women, for writers of color, for parents, for LGBTQ writers, and writers with disabilities. There are famous retreats such as Bread Loaf and Sewanee that feature big name faculty, highly competitive admissions, and fees into the thousands of dollars. But there are also scores of regional retreats with highly qualified faculty and much less sticker shock (the Green Mountain Writers Conference in Vermont, for instance, offers a five-day conference for about a third the per-day price of Bread Loaf). Any retreat will offer the opportunity to meet other writers and get feedback on specific projects.

The writing residency: Residencies offer writers a private, quiet space to work unencumbered by everyday distractions. Some residencies are short (just a few days) while others can last months. Some offer hot meals, gigabit Internet, and evening activities, and some offer nothing but a solar-powered cabin in the middle of the woods. Some offer stipends and scholarships while others are completely free but their admission is highly competitive. Some include small teaching requirements or public reading obligations while others leave writers entirely to themselves. Where conferences and retreats are about getting energized by the writing community, making friends, discovering new ideas, and receiving helpful feedback, residencies are about one thing—the blank page, and time to fill it.

Which Is Best?

In a perfect world, we'd have access to a writing residency any time we needed it, and we'd have occasional retreats to gather feedback. And then we could go to conferences and pitch our bright, shiny manuscripts to all those eager editors and publishers just waiting for our next masterpiece.

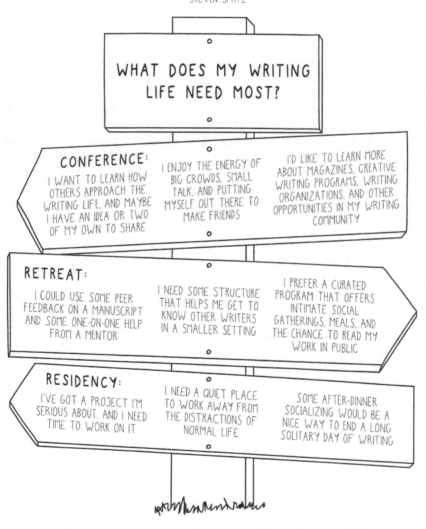

CONFERENCE, RETREAT, OR RESIDENCY?

"IT'S INVIGORATING TO BE SURROUNDED BY OTHER WRITERS – ALL THAT ENERGY, HOPE, AND DETERMINATION IS LIKE A KIND OF ELECTRICITY BUZZING IN THE AIR."
– STEVEN SPATZ

WHAT DOES MY WRITING LIFE NEED MOST?

CONFERENCE:
I WANT TO LEARN HOW OTHERS APPROACH THE WRITING LIFE, AND MAYBE I HAVE AN IDEA OR TWO OF MY OWN TO SHARE

I ENJOY THE ENERGY OF BIG CROWDS, SMALL TALK, AND PUTTING MYSELF OUT THERE TO MAKE FRIENDS

I'D LIKE TO LEARN MORE ABOUT MAGAZINES, CREATIVE WRITING PROGRAMS, WRITING ORGANIZATIONS, AND OTHER OPPORTUNITIES IN MY WRITING COMMUNITY

RETREAT:
I COULD USE SOME PEER FEEDBACK ON A MANUSCRIPT AND SOME ONE-ON-ONE HELP FROM A MENTOR

I NEED SOME STRUCTURE THAT HELPS ME GET TO KNOW OTHER WRITERS IN A SMALLER SETTING

I PREFER A CURATED PROGRAM THAT OFFERS INTIMATE SOCIAL GATHERINGS, MEALS, AND THE CHANCE TO READ MY WORK IN PUBLIC

RESIDENCY:
I'VE GOT A PROJECT I'M SERIOUS ABOUT, AND I NEED TIME TO WORK ON IT

I NEED A QUIET PLACE TO WORK AWAY FROM THE DISTRACTIONS OF NORMAL LIFE

SOME AFTER-DINNER SOCIALIZING WOULD BE A NICE WAY TO END A LONG SOLITARY DAY OF WRITING

FIGURE 5 *"Conference, Retreat, or Residency?" with an epigraph from Steven Spatz, "Every Writer Should Attend at Least One Conference," Book Baby, March 1, 2022, https://blog.bookbaby.com/2018/06/every-writer-should-attend-at-least -one-writers-conference (used with permission).*

But alas, we all operate on limited time and money, so we have to pick and choose.

According to blogger Jason Brick, the conference/retreat/residency question is not about better or worse but about "which works best for you right now." And the answer to that question depends a great deal on what we're working on. "It's worse to go to a writer's conference when your work needs the detailed focus of a [retreat]," writes Brick. Or it might be worse "to spend the time and money on a [retreat] when what you need is a conference."[1] Even worse? To show up at a residency with nothing to work on, or to kill time and waste money at a conference when we should really be using that long weekend to hammer out the next chapter of our novel. I like Brick's question, but in a slightly different form: "What does my writing life need most right now?"

If we need an introduction to the larger writing community and the inspiration that comes from hearing lots of writers talk about their work, then a conference may be the right choice (especially if we love small talk in a big crowd). If what we need is one-on-one mentorship and the synergy that comes from working alongside other writers, then a retreat might be better. And if all we really need is some time and space to write, then conferences and retreats are overkill. Sign up for a residency, skip all (or most) of the socializing, and get to writing.

Finding the Right Fit

Poets & Writers Magazine (pw.org) and the AWP (awpwriter.org) both curate extensive, up-to-date, easily searchable databases of nearly every conference, retreat, or residency in the English-speaking world (and then some). Searches can be narrowed by genre, region, and event type, and listings include brief descriptions, contact links, and funding information.

Also consider talking to mentors and other writers. They will likely know of and may even have contacts at local and regional events, and any writer who has been to a conference, retreat, or residency will likely have strong opinions about which to consider (and which to avoid).

It will take some research to find the right event. There's cost to consider, and scheduling, but beyond those practical concerns is the question of fit. For conferences and retreats, travel writer Don George recommends that we "google the writers, editors and agents [who will be featured at the conference] and [get] a good sense of what they've written, what kind of publications they edit and what kinds of writers they represent."[2] Not only does this help us narrow down our search, but according to George, it helps prepare us for when we actually meet those we've researched: "Writers, editors and agents really appreciate it when the students they speak with are already familiar with their work."

And don't put too much stock in celebrity instructors. "Here's the thing about the big fishes," says Courtney Maum. "The big fishes are tired. This is the one hundred and eleventh literary conference they have taught at this year. Sometimes, you're better off taking a workshop with the underdogs."[3] Maum suggests doing some online research to figure out who has studied with potential teachers. "Be that crazy person who Facebook messages total strangers to ask what their workshop experience was like." One of my most helpful mentors has never published a book, but her skill as an editor and reader are unrivaled, and I'd recommend her as a workshop leader over just about anyone I know. In the end, it's solid mentorship and not proximity to celebrity that will help improve our writing.

There's another, perhaps more urgent, question that gets beyond professional or aesthetic compatibility. As we've discussed in previous chapters, the writing community can be a fairly white, middle-class, heteronormative, able-bodied place, and for writers from traditionally marginalized groups, these events can either exacerbate feelings of othering or they can foster feelings of inclusion. One solution is to look for events that aim to elevate underrepresented voices. In addition to retreats and conferences for specific groups (see Chapter 4 section on identity-based mentoring for some sponsoring organizations), many general audience programs include principles of diversity in their mission statements.

But, says poet Sandra Beasley, giving lip-service to diversity is not the same as supporting it: "If a program specifically solicits applications from a marginalized community of which you are a member, take a close look at why,"[4] writes Beasley. It may be that the organization is "genuinely welcoming, and they want to get the word out to more people," or they may be trying to check off a diversity box. If it's the latter, Beasley warns, "you might feel isolated or tokenized, and you'll probably have to do some work of educating." To find out more about a particular program's inclusivity practices, contact the organization directly, or better yet, talk to previous attendees (look for names mentioned on a program's website, or ask the program manager for a few contacts). Given the value of community support to a successful writing life, it's worth taking the time to find the right fit.

Completing an Application

Each event will list its own set of application requirements on its website, but there are some basics worth touching on briefly.

Conference presentation proposals: To attend a conference, one simply pays the registration fee and shows up, but many conferences want attendees to present work, and that typically requires some kind of proposal. Panel topics might include anything from literary citizenship and marketing to craft, theory, criticism, and pedagogy.

Some conferences ask for individual paper abstracts that they then group with three to five other proposals to form various panel discussions. Other conferences require applicants to organize themselves into groups first and then propose a panel together. The Western Literature Association Conference, for example, accepts proposals for creative work presentations made up of four fifteen-minute performances, and they ask for a 150–200 word abstract.[5] The AWP conference asks for a 500-character event description and a 500-character statement of merit.[6] NonfictioNow, an international conference, describes their ideal panel as "a lively, discursive, playful, and interactive event, as opposed to the reading of a succession of individual papers."[7]

Many conferences consider diversity and inclusion when planning their programs. According to their website, AWP "seeks proposals featuring panelists who are diverse in their backgrounds, pursuits, affiliations, and ages," and NonfictioNow aims for panels that "include a diverse group of participants, reflecting the inclusive and international nature" of the conference. There aren't quotas or specific diversity requirements for panels, but as the AWP says in their panel proposal guidelines, "An event that demonstrates interscholastic play, inter-generational collaboration, and diversity has a far greater chance of appealing to a large audience and providing an issue with the lively analysis it deserves."[8] For more specific advice on panel proposals, it is best to check with each organization's proposal guidelines and with previous presenters (and you can also see joeyfranklin.com/writershustle for examples).

Retreats and residencies: Whether it's a workshop-heavy retreat or a solo residency in the woods, most programs will ask for both a writing sample and a short letter of intent. Organizers want to know where we are at in our progress as writers and how ready we are to make the most of the time, space, and resources they provide.

The writing sample: This should highlight not only our ability to write a sentence but also our ability to think deeply, and engage with ideas that matter. If there's a page limit, less is always better than more. If it's hard to decide which sample to send, consider asking a friend or mentor to look over possible manuscripts.

The letter of intent: We should be specific about our goals. If we hope to complete a 10,000-word first chapter or revise an entire manuscript or get feedback on a poem sequence, we should state that from the beginning. But the letter of intent is not a contract. Event organizers know that plans change. The goal is to demonstrate that we've thought clearly about our work and that we're intentional about how we plan to use our time.

Preparing for the Trip

Once we've decided on an event, and once we've applied and been accepted, the real work begins. To make the most of the time and money we're spending, there are few principles to consider:

Set Goals

Whether we're at a convention center for the weekend with 13,000 other writers, or all by ourselves in a cabin in Vermont for a month, setting goals helps use make the most of our time.

At a **conference** such as AWP, our goals might be focused on information and idea gathering, or on getting to know other people. Before my graduate students leave for a conference, I give them three challenges: get to know at least three other writers, learn something new about a literary market they're interested in, and come home with twenty new ideas. With such goals in mind, we can more easily choose which panels to attend and which to skip, and we give ourselves some clarity about the kinds of relationships we're looking to build with the people we meet.

Goals at a **retreat** can be focused on inspiration and people (definitely bring a notebook to jot things down, and take the time to connect with folks on social media), but given the emphasis on workshops and writing time, we ought to have some kind of manuscript goal. If the retreat lasts only a few days, we might bring something to revise. If we've got a week or two, we might plan to start something from scratch. Knowing what we want to work on will make writing time more generative and workshops more useful.

In the case of **residencies**, preparing a specific plan is typically part of the application process. But once we're on site, it will take daily goals to bring those plans to fruition. We might make word- or page-count goals, or set specific time goals. But we can also make reading goals, research goals, or even exercise goals—whatever helps us invest more fully in our writing. If a residency offers weekly open-mic nights or other opportunities to share work, consider turning those events into soft deadlines for having something ready to read.

Establish a Simple Online Presence

Some writers still use business cards, but it's just as common to simply exchange emails and point one another to online portfolios. So, writes Julie Zigoris, "If you have a website, make sure it's up to date."[9] She also recommends updating all our social media accounts and even putting our own names into Google to see what comes up. Having a simple, professional online presence is as important as taking a shower and brushing our teeth.

But think twice before getting carried away. An author website should be easy to navigate, easy to maintain, and easy to afford. It may be helpful to think of an author website as a digital business card. Include contact information, maybe a photograph and a short bio, and links to some writing samples. But beyond that, be wary of blogs or other content that requires upkeep. Dynamic content can theoretically drive traffic to our websites, but updating all that content can take time, and we should only worry about website content if it helps us with our other writing goals.

Get Out of Your Comfort Zone

Being a first-time attendee can feel a bit like crashing someone else's high school reunion. Everybody knows everybody else, and it's easy to disappear into the crowd if we aren't willing to extend ourselves a bit. "That doesn't mean you have to be the life of the party," says Bob Hostetler. "Just that you work a little harder to introduce yourself, strike up conversations, and ask questions."[10] Ask folks what they're working on. Ask about what they're reading. Find out what events they've been enjoying. Commiserate about the writing life. Even talking to one more person than we normally would is a good start. Two is even better.

Consider Volunteering

Most conferences, retreats, and residencies are run by nonprofit entities, educational organizations, or arts centers, and many rely heavily on volunteer work. Some even offer volunteers discounts or other perks in exchange for help. But as nice as a registration discount might be, the real reason to volunteer, writes Cathy C. Hall, is "because you will meet other people."[11] Whether we're helping out with food, registration, or ushering, we'll inevitably end up working alongside other volunteers, and that's an easy recipe for making friends. As Hall puts it, "volunteering gets you inside the conference instead of sitting on the sidelines."

Make Friends, Not Contacts

New writers, in addition to feeling lonely, can often be quite hungry for professional contacts. But we can't let that hunger transform our mingling into a careerist version of speed-dating: rushing through small talk to find out if someone can be helpful to us and then moving on if we decide they're not. At a conference this might manifest itself as incessant name-tag checking ("Have I heard of this person?") or looking over people's shoulders for someone more interesting. At a retreat it might be more subtle—spending all our time talking with the faculty instead of other attendees or simply keeping to ourselves because we don't think we have anything to gain from other people. Freelancer John Peragine practices a magnanimous approach: "When I meet someone [at a writing event], I listen to them. I think about ways I can help them."[12] To Peragine, networking situations are "about getting to know the other person. You cannot possibly do that if you are dominating the conversation . . . Give others a chance to open up, and eventually they will come around and ask about you."

And Brian Klems reminds us that after making friends, the next step is to follow up. "When you get home, send a little two- to three-line 'so glad to have met you' email, and then stay in touch with the writers you met."[13] The only caveat I'd add is that follow-up should be natural. If we have a question or want to thank someone for a good conversation or advice, or perhaps express interest in further collaboration, go ahead and send that email. If an editor or agent invites us to submit something to them, we better make that our first priority. But mere "networking" emails can end up being more alienating than anything.

Go to Panels and Other Program Events, but Not Too Many

This advice comes from poet Rich Smith, who wrote a few years ago about his "guerilla-style approach" to attending conferences: advice that includes hanging out at nearby bars, sneaking into the bookfair, and skipping panels. "Some panels are great," he writes. "But mostly they're just CV-stuffing exercises that most people write on the plane."[14] Having written such panel presentations myself and having been in the audience at dozens of really good ones, I've got to call foul on Smith's hyperbole, but he still makes a valid point. If we stick to nothing but preplanned events, we're missing out on half the magic. Smith recommends unofficial events that "are free, in bars, open to the public" and "stacked with emerging and established talent." The best part, according to Smith: "You can leave in the middle of one without the whole room giving you the stink-eye."

To Smith's advice on off-site events, I'd add a recommendation to see the city. Walk along the waterfront if there is one; take in a museum or a park. Maybe even catch a show. Spend an hour in a quiet coffee shop, bookstore, or library. Take advantage of the time away from home and soak in the inspiration of a new city.

If You're Working on a Book, Be Ready to Pitch

Writing events can be an excellent place to get the attention of editors and agents, and if we're ready to market a book we ought to prepare ourselves to pitch it in a flash. Try to summarize the book in just a sentence or two.

Be sure to answer two important questions: What's the book about, and why would someone want to read it? Don't worry about all the details. Think big-picture issues and urgent questions. It might be helpful to imagine pitching books by well-known authors. How might we describe in one enticing sentence a book such as *H Is for Hawk* by Helen McDonald or *The Underground Railroad* by Colson Whitehead? Then, once we've got a solid sentence or two, Kerrie Flanagan suggests we practice the pitch so we can "present it in a way that is more conversational." She recommends trying a pitch on family or friends. "Get some feedback on what each person liked and didn't like. Incorporate the relevant feedback, practice a little more, [and] then trust that you are ready to go."[15]

Don't Overdo It

Conferences and retreats can be physically and emotionally draining. Just getting around can mean a lot more walking than we're used to, but there's also the mental effort of listening, taking notes, chatting with strangers, and even performing. Being "on" for too long can take its toll. "It can be difficult to have downtime between all the events and panels," says Julie Zigoris. "Don't try to attend everything—rest is essential."[16] We have to give ourselves permission to get away from the crowds and find a way to recharge. Lots of writers swear by late night bar talk, but it isn't a must, at least not every night. We ought to pick and choose what will really be helpful and get comfortable with saying "no" when we need to.

Budget Smart

Writers affiliated with a university, be they graduate students or faculty, can often get some kind of help with the cost of conferences or retreats, but lacking a professional affiliation shouldn't bar us from finding meaningful events to participate in. Unless we're attending something local, the major costs are usually airfare and lodging. If a conference is within driving distance, consider carpooling with other writers to cut costs. Likewise, sharing an Airbnb or hotel or staying at a hostel—or, if we're feeling really adventurous (or broke), using a service such as couchsurfing.com can be another way to save money (surf at your own risk).

I've done all of these, and while staying at the conference hotel has its perks, more creative approaches to housing usually make for better stories (ask me or Pat Madden sometime about an AirBnB in Flagstaff, Arizona, with saloon doors on its bathroom). Some conferences and retreats offer volunteer discounts or scholarships based on need or merit. And most of the time, food can be found for pretty cheap—think breakfast sandwiches from Dunkin' and Subway for dinner (though I recommend reserving a little cash for at least one sit-down meal with a new friend or potential collaborator—

such mealtime conversations are priceless). And if big national events are out of the question, start with a more accessible, often cheaper local one, or double up a conference trip and a vacation to get more for your travel money.

A CONFERENCE, RETREAT, OR RESIDENCY can help us take important next steps in our writing, but books don't get written when we're out meeting new people. If we let events become too much of a priority, we end up with lots of friends and not much writing to show for it. In general, it's best to temper our expectations about what these events can and can't do for us and to even consider alternatives.

For instance, if attending a formal retreat is simply out of the question, consider the do-it-yourself approach. Booking a hotel room in the next town over or even holing up in the library on a Saturday can create ample opportunity for getting work done, especially if we coax a friend to join us who is as eager for the focused writing time as we are. Graduate students in the program I help run recently held their own winter retreat at someone's family cabin. They all pitched in for food, headed into the mountains, and spent their weekend working on their projects, and occasionally heading out to play in the snow.

The basic ingredients of a makeshift retreat, says writing coach Cathy Mazak, are (1) altering our physical space ("you could go to your public library, you could go to a hotel lobby; you could go to a coffee shop in a nearby town"); (2) making a plan for physical needs (get someone to watch the dog or the kids, and figure out what to do for meals); and (3) implementing some kind of structure. For one client, Mazak created a simple plan for her DIY retreat: "Write. Walk. Eat. Write Walk. Eat. [The client] would do an hour or an hour and a half of writing . . . then she would take a thirty minute walk. Then she'd have a snack or a meal. And then she would cycle through that again."[17] Even if we don't have any money to spare, with a little out-of-the-box thinking we can open up some space in our busy schedules for the writing life and our work will be the better for it.

And finally, if we aren't able to accomplish all of our goals, don't take it too hard. During her first writing retreat, Marisa Mohi remembers feeling overwhelmed by imposter syndrome. "Because uninterrupted time is so hard to come by, I felt that I should be spending my days at the retreat working on the Next Great American Novel."[18] Instead, she spent a lot of time feeling unqualified to write anything. "Don't waste time worrying that you're wasting time with the words that are coming out," she says. Rather, just "get to typin'." And we might consider similar advice for other events. It's very likely that we'll end up sitting through an unhelpful panel, wandering aimlessly through a book fair, or spending an afternoon staring at the wood grain in our desks without feeling like we're accomplishing anything. It's okay to cut ourselves some slack. Bottom line: be friendly, take notes, have fun, say yes. Even when things don't go quite right, they'll never go entirely wrong.

6.

FINISHING PROJECTS

In the early days of the Covid-19 pandemic, some writers were fond of reminding everyone on social media that Shakespeare had written *King Lear* during the plague and that while on lockdown Sir Isaac Newton had invented calculus. *No excuses!* these posts seemed to say. *You're not going to let a pandemic keep you from writing, are you?* Others took the opposite tack: *Sure you had ice cream for breakfast, but you put on pants for that Zoom meeting. Take the win!* And while the former mindset smacks of a certain privilege (Shakespeare and Newton weren't tending children, and someone else cooked their meals), the latter risks lowering the bar so far as to excuse us from accomplishing anything (Is putting on pants really worth celebrating?). Neither approach alone is much help, but together they reveal two important facts of the writing life: First, that every writer who wants to complete a project must do so in the face of life's other demands—a day job, family life, health issues, and yes, occasionally a global pandemic. And second, that part of working through those other demands means forgiving ourselves when life gets in the way.

Perhaps we're in a workshop with a deadline just a few weeks away. Maybe we're in a graduate program and we're thinking about a thesis or dissertation. Maybe we work full-time and only have nights and weekends to finish our novel, but we're stuck on Chapter 5. Large or small, simple or complex, all writing projects begin with work. There's no substitute for keeping ourselves at the keyboard, but by combining some practical project management skills with some fundamental composition strategies, we can make the most of that keyboard time and in the process accomplish more of our writing goals more often.

Prioritize the Work

While writing her first novel, *Lunatic in My Head*,[1] Anjum Hasan discovered that part of the "real work of being a writer" was not just feeling one's way into a story, but having the discipline to "submit oneself" to the project every day, even when one doesn't feel like writing. She introduced me to the Urdu/ Arabic word *riyaaz*, which means something like "regular practice," but, as Hasan explains, "also suggests practice itself as a kind of lifestyle." What Hasan has discovered—what every writer must discover for themselves—is that writing is not only about having something to say but about "getting one's body to sit in that chair, getting one's fingers to move on that keyboard, compelling oneself to read what one has written, trying every day to find a strand in it that one can continue weaving with."[2]

So how do we do that? We set specific, realistic, measurable goals and set deadlines for ourselves to complete them. We hold ourselves accountable for the goals and deadlines we've set, and then we reward ourselves for making progress. Such an easy couple of sentences to write, but these principles take real hustle to implement.

Set Goals and Deadlines

For screenwriter Tom Provost, finding time to write is the biggest obstacle: "It can be very easy to make writing the last thing on my to-do list, which means it often falls by the wayside."[3] He recommends measurable goals related directly to the writing—a page a day for those just starting out. But, he says, "each writer has to figure out for themselves what works best." Poets, for instance, tend to care less about page- or word-counts, so a time-based goal might be better for them. Whether we commit to writing a page a day or an hour a day, putting that goal at the top of our to-do list will set us up to make real progress.

What's better than a goal? A goal with a deadline. "Deadlines bring focus," writes National Novel Writing Month founder Chris Baty. He thinks of deadlines as "enthusiastic shepherds adept at plucking the mini inspirations that lurk in the wings of our imaginations and flinging them bodily into the bright light of day."[4] Consider how a goal and a deadline transform the following writerly aspirations into real possibilities:

Aspiration	+ Goal	+ Deadline
Someday I will write a novel.	*I will work on my novel for three hours every day.*	*I will work on my novel for three hours every day and have a draft completed by December.*
I'd sure like to publish a poem.	*I will write one poem a month this winter.*	*I will write one poem a month this winter and submit four poems to the* New England Review *by their May 1 deadline.*
I've got this great idea for an essay.	*I will write 500 words a day.*	*I will write 500 words a day and complete an essay draft by next Friday to share with my writing group.*

The magic of the goal-plus-deadline formula is twofold. First, because goals give us a regular target to aim at, we'll almost always produce more with a goal than without. And second, because we have a deadline to work toward, we're more likely to finish projects. And even if we miss a deadline, it doubles as a project management checkpoint—a moment for us to reevaluate and recommit to goals and keep moving forward.

Create a Routine

Our goals are easier to accomplish when we develop a regular schedule that considers how writing fits into the rest of our lives. Novelist Haruki Murakami is famous for his rigorous routine. "I get up at four a.m. And work for five to six hours," he told *The Paris Review* in 2004. "In the afternoon, I run for ten kilometers or swim for fifteen hundred meters (or do both), then I read a bit and listen to some music."[5] He's in bed each night by 9 pm, and he repeats this schedule, day in and day out, for months at a time. Such a routine "requires a good amount of mental and physical strength," says Murakami. "Writing a novel is like survival training. Physical strength is as necessary as artistic sensitivity."

But routines are just as helpful for shorter projects. Poet Kimberly Johnson writes on the run, literally. "When I'm working on a poem, if I write a line a day I'm on fire. So it's not really a burden to carry three or five or seven words along with me in my head, rearranging them, making substitutions, expanding and erasing until the line does whatever work it needs to do." She runs mostly in the evenings, usually around the streets of the Sugar House neighborhood in Salt Lake City, but her pavement-pounding practice is not merely a matter of convenience. "My peculiar writing process has the advantage of keeping my attention on patterns," she explains. "My breath and the rhythm of my feet ensure that I'm aware of the body and of the kinds of recurrences that profit a line of poetry: metrical patterning, the repetition of vowels and consonants, the relationship between phrases and pauses."[6]

University of San Francisco professor Kirstin Chen encourages her students to set goals that fit their lives. A confirmed night owl, for instance, probably shouldn't set lofty early morning writing goals. "Instead of fighting their natural instincts, writers should lean in to them and do whatever they can to schedule their lives around their preferred work style."[7] And it's also okay if routines change. In fact, changing routines might even be necessary. "Sometimes muscles can atrophy in a routine," says poet Michael Lavers. "We need something to force us out of that comfort zone." For Lavers this means that once a month he gets off his computer and does all his writing longhand "because something different happens" when he's using a pen and paper. "As valuable as routines are, some strategic disruption can help keep us flexible."[8]

And what works today may not be a routine at all. When poet ire'ne lara silva started writing seriously, she had little room in her schedule, or her home, for her work. "I learned to carry a composition notebook everywhere I went. I learned to write while I was on the bus, waiting in line at the pharmacy or the grocery store. I wrote on work breaks and during lunch hours. I wrote late at night. I wrote in every corner of the day."[9] She eventually came to the conclusion that it was okay to "give" herself time to write, rather than stealing it from the rest of her life. And for silva, that meant also giving herself time to rest, and to day dream, and to even do nothing. "In the end, it's not about discipline or time management," says silva. "It's about safeguarding your energy and being generous with yourself." What matters, finally, is that we find our own approach and stick to it until it no longer helps. Then we find another one and keep going. Wash. Rinse. Repeat.

Be Accountable

Goals and routines work only if we follow them, and that's easier to do if we report our progress to somebody. That might be as simple as reporting to ourselves in a diary or journal (*Today I wrote 500 words*), but some form of public reporting will likely keep us more honest. Freelance writer Tonya Abari lives by her goals, and she reviews them daily, weekly, and at the end of each quarter. But what makes her goals work are her accountability partners. During the Covid-19 pandemic, Abari participated in several virtual write-ins where she and her writing partners logged in to Zoom and wrote together. "My writing partners are people who I can have open conversations about goal setting with. We always check in with each other and talk about ways in which we can better accomplish our goals."[10]

When I first started out as a professor, I exchanged goals with a colleague and we met for lunch once a month to talk shop. Later on I started posting a word-count goal outside my office along with one of those thermometer charts that I could fill in each day indicating my progress. That wasn't a report so much as a (slightly corny) public stunt to keep myself honest. However, fewer things have been more motivating than knowing a colleague might see that chart and ask me about my progress.

Reward Yourself

If we want to make our routines easier to stick with, we've got to reward ourselves in the process. "I let myself listen to an audio book and work in the garden if I get 1000 words,"[11] says YA novelist Ann Dee Ellis. And she's used lots of other rewards too: going for a hike, pausing work for a quick show on Netflix, or even something as simple as eating lunch. "I set small goals and small rewards that keep me moving forward."

If we really want to turn our routines into long-term habits though, we have to get more neurologically precise with our rewards. According to behavior scientist B. J. Fogg, it all comes down to dopamine, the neurotransmitter that "controls the brain's 'reward system' and helps us remember what behavior led to feeling good so we will do it again."[12] But our brains aren't going to create the neurochemical connection between behavior and reward unless the reward comes right on the heels of the behavior. Again, Fogg: "Doing three squats in the morning and rewarding yourself with a movie that evening won't work to rewire your brain. The squats and the good feelings you get from the movie are too far apart for dopamine to build a bridge between the two."

To chemically cement our routines, writes Fogg, we need immediate rewards. "You've got to celebrate right after the behavior . . . and you need your celebration to feel real." It may sound silly, but simply saying *Yes!* and adding a fist pump can do it. Or clapping your hands or even just smiling. My favorite of Fogg's recommendations: "look up and make a V with your arms."[13] What might change if we treated every finished paragraph like a touchdown? Every complete chapter like the final notes of a symphony? Every "The End" like a curtain call?

Writing coach Bec Evans offers a final important word of advice about rewards. "The amount of effort you put into writing can't always be measured by word count. Sometimes writing in short energetic bursts can move your work on in leaps and bounds. Other days you spend hours and barely produce a workable paragraph. So, reward the effort you put in, not the outcome."[14] Simply put, if we've got a two-hour-a-day writing goal but only manage thirty minutes, go ahead and throw that victory V in the air. It's the work that deserves celebrating, not perfection.

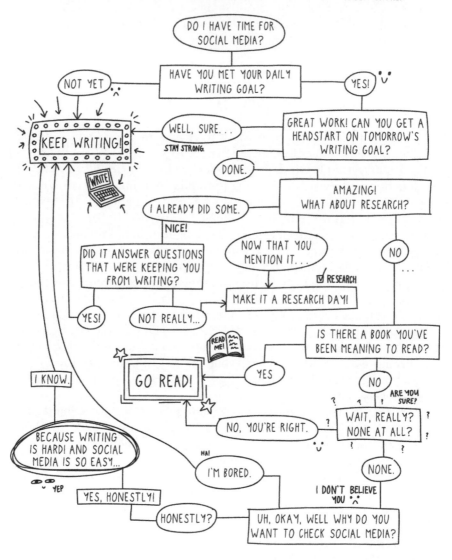

FIGURE 6 *"To Scroll or Not to Scroll?" with an epigraph from Willa Cather, "State Laws Are Cramping,"* Lincoln Evening State Journal, *31 October 1921, https:// cather.unl.edu/writings/bohlke/speeches/bohlke.s.03.*

Trust the Process

Hearing some writers describe their process, we might be forgiven for assuming they've joined a cult. Take Ian Rankin, who says, "I'm really not in control at all of what I'm writing. It's almost as though before I start . . . there's a shape sitting there that I've not seen yet, and when I start to write the novel the shape will reveal itself to me."[15] Erika Sanchez says something similar about her poetry: "I know it sounds new agey and kind of mystical, but the poems tell me what they want."[16] And Stephen King writes that "good story ideas seem to come quite literally from nowhere, sailing at you right out of the empty sky."[17] So many writers use similar language, and while it may indeed sound "new agey and kind of mystical," in reality, the entire process is much more human. George Saunders tells us that "the real experience of writing . . . is made up of thousands of tiny intuitive leaps."[18] What seems mysterious is actually just our brains at work, and when we work within a routine, we're merely exercising the patience necessary to move from one of those tiny leaps to the next.

So we put down words and then pause. We put down a few more words and then see where that gets us. We stop to reread. Maybe we cut something out, or a particular image or idea conjures something new, and we write that down. We finish for the day, and then start again in the morning. One word, one sentence, one day at a time, we move forward, searching for the right language. "Writing should always be exploratory," says Marilynne Robinson. "There shouldn't be the assumption that you know ahead of time what you want to express. When you enter into the dance with language, you'll begin to find that there's something before, or behind, or more absolute than the thing you thought you wanted to express. And as you work, other kinds of meaning emerge than what you might have expected."[19]

Consider poet Jericho Brown, whose work is rich in cultural criticism but often begins as little more than sounds that Brown finds "musically attractive." "I try to transliterate those sounds into lines and follow them with lines that riff off of the sounds of those lines," explains Brown. "I don't concern myself with sense, at first."[20] To Brown, trusting the process means following the sound and knowing that meaningfulness will eventually come.

For memoirist Lauren Kay Johnson, *the process* starts out as "an effort to understand something, work through an idea, or just make something tangible out of a mass of jumbled thoughts."[21] But in "making something tangible" out of her thoughts she's preparing a textual foundation to build on later. And it doesn't matter if her ideas are disorganized, incomplete, or only partially formed. She knows that the polished draft of tomorrow will never happen without the messy experimentation of today.

Manage Writer's Block

It has become fashionable in some corners of the Internet to suggest that writer's block isn't a thing. If we find ourselves stuck on a project, we're either lazy,[22] mentally weak[23] or treating writing too much like a hobby.[24] But for even the most rigorous, committed writers, inspiration occasionally wanes, doubts begin to fester, and we find ourselves in a writing rut. What do we do then? There's no magic bullet for writer's block, but there are ways we can refocus, jump-start our creative juices, and remind ourselves of why we're writing in the first place.

Draft a Theme Statement

For prose writers, story guru Robert McKee suggests condensing a project down to "one clear, coherent sentence that expresses a story's meaning."[25] Such a theme statement can help us discover what a story is really about, and it can help get us back on track if we ever veer too far from our thematic throughline.

For many poets, the idea of a theme statement may be anathema to their composition practice, but most will cop to the idea that at some point, reflection is in order. After his initial attention to "what things sound like," Jericho Brown then asks his text several questions. "Who are you? What is your personality? How do you feel? Who is your speaker? What is your tone of voice? Why are you talking now? What has led to this moment for you?" These questions help Brown move from his initial love of sound "toward sense and writing what becomes a first draft."[26]

Consider an Outline

Outlines aren't for everyone, but many writers, especially storytellers trying to manage a complex plot or argumentative throughline, rely on outlines to keep moving in the right direction. "I am a big fan of outlining," writes A. J. Jacobs. "I write an outline. Then a slightly more detailed outline. Then another with even more detail. Sentences form, punctuation is added, and eventually it all turns into a book."[27]

Another unrepentant outliner is novelist Brandon Sanderson. "I feel lost in a story if I don't have a climax in mind," writes Sanderson. "And I have trouble writing a character if I don't know where [or] how they are supposed to progress."[28] That said, he recognizes that an outline can be a crutch. Instead of a complete, detailed outline, Sanderson uses what he calls a "points on the map" approach, which involves identifying several key moments in a project and using them as guides, writing from one point to another, and building up a story as he goes. According to Sanderson, "this is a good way to have some of the organization of an outline without losing spontaneity."

Read Your Way Out

For short story writer Daisy Johnson, picking up a book always helps with writer's block. "Whenever I'm stuck I pick up a book and, if it's good, after a couple of sentences I'll be back in the zone again."[29] That "zone," I think, is the zone of well-wrought words on the page. Just being with the finely crafted ideas of another writer can prime us for our own work. As poet Maggie Smith puts it, "spending time with beautiful sentences day after day gives a writer an intuitive sense of syntax, structure, and turn."[30]

Turn Your Problem into "The Story"

In an interview with *Image Journal*, Leslie Jamison recalls a student who'd been a professional snowboarder and was struggling with how to write about surviving an avalanche. The student complained to Jamison, "People keep telling me this is the most boring avalanche they've ever read," and that got Jamison fired up. "I told [the student], 'This isn't a problem, this is the point! Part of your subject is that trauma isn't always hyper-dramatic. It isn't always an amazing story.'"[31] Jamison identifies an important strategy— turn potential liabilities into assets. Struggling to remember the details of a traumatic event? Make that struggle part of the story. Got a developing novel with two competing narrators? Consider telling the story from two points of view. Has a poem's argumentative or musical progression gotten lost in the weeds of familiar language or tired images? Before backtracking, take a good look around and see if those weeds could be cultivated into their own music.

Embrace the Difficulty

For all our worry about writer's block, it may be that feeling "stuck" isn't the problem we think it is. As poet ire'ne lara silva tells me: "I think writing should be difficult. If I'm not writing the most difficult, most vulnerable, most confounding things possible, then I'm not doing my job."[32] If we find ourselves struggling with what to say, it may mean that we need to clear the cobwebs from our mind or refocus ourselves on what's most thematically important. We may need to consider an outline or read our way out of trouble, but trouble itself may simply mean that we're engaged in the difficult, important work of saying something honest and vital. Getting ourselves unstuck may ultimately mean giving ourselves permission to write the hard things that need to be written.

Lean into Feedback

So much of what's necessary to tackle any creative writing project is personal. The audacity to assume that we have something worth saying, the courage to put that something on the page, the discipline to keep writing, revising, cutting and shaping until a story emerges, or a persona comes to life, or a stanza hums with music and meaning. But for all that essential individual effort, even the best writer eventually needs a frank, honest reader—a fellow lover of language and ideas who can help us cut through sentimentality and self-indulgence, who can show us our blind spots and sometimes help us understand what we're really trying to say.

Who do we ask, though? Leslie Wibberley suggests we look for readers within our target audience: "genre, age category, interests, and even gender" are all things to consider. "It won't serve you as well to ask someone who only enjoys hard science fiction to read your romance novel, or to ask a romance reader to read a high fantasy story."[33] On the other hand, "don't discount the perspective of a smart reader who doesn't share your aesthetic," says Anne Pancake. "Because I understand style a lot better than I understand plot, I can learn a lot from good readers who grasp plot better than the intricacies of language."[34] And for Sheila Heti, it's important to get more than one early reader. "What if you show it to only one person and they hate it? And you believe them! Or they love it? And you believe them! Better to send it to two, three or four people, so that you can situate the truth about the draft somewhere along that range."[35]

The timing of feedback is also important. Poet Lisa Olstein prefers "to be down in the dirt" with her projects before showing them to other people. "As a poem develops, its animating energy, voice, and means of discovery can be so easily interrupted, almost spooked,"[36] says Olstein. Part of her process involves protecting the creative, generative space of the poem "until it's well enough embodied not to be too easily thrown off course." Then she's happy to show it to other people, to "cut or reorder or otherwise muck around with it." Likewise, Salman Rushdie prefers to take a project "as far as he can" before showing it to anyone. "It's not so much about needing them to like it," he continues. "What I really want is for them to tell me where the problems are . . .You need nonsycophantic people who will tell you the truth."[37]

Of course, for some of us, honest feedback can be debilitating. But it hurts less if we can find a way to see it more objectively. Tanaz Bhathena suggests we treat feedback the way we treat our early drafts: "Let [the feedback] sit in a drawer for a few weeks before picking it up again to see it with fresh eyes."[38] On a first reading, a critique might sting a little, but, says Bhathena, "when looked at two weeks after it's given, can sometimes make a lot more sense."

The hardest kind of criticism to process is when different readers come to different conclusions about our work. Ann Pancake's suggestion: "When you hear conflicting advice about a single issue, consider the source of the criticism and listen to your gut."[39] Perhaps conflicting responses from readers is a good thing, says Pancake. "Two readers taking notice of the same element of your story in different ways may mean that you're actually doing something right there—something unusual or unexpected." Then again, conflicting responses may indicate that readers have discovered a hot spot in the text—a line, image, paragraph or scene that needs some kind of attention.

Some feedback is decidedly easier to accept than others. Praise is always nice (writing is hard, after all), but, as Leigh Shulman tells us, "the most wonderful, full-of-praise positive feedback is worthless if it doesn't help you know what to do next."[40] We should take all praise with a grain of salt, especially if it doesn't at least imply ways of improving our manuscript. And when we do get a good suggestion for improvement, we should embrace it, even if temporarily. "Oftentimes, students will respond to a critique by trying to do the smallest amount possible," writes Susan Breen. "They cling to the manuscript as though it were a life preserver and shave off little bits and pieces of it." But art doesn't favor the timid. "Be bold. Shake it up," she suggests. "This is your opportunity to do something really special."[41] Even if we don't ultimately use a suggestion, giving it a test drive in revision can help us see our work more clearly.

And finally, Scott Francis reminds us not to get overwhelmed by feedback, especially when it's overloaded with criticism. "Everyone has an opinion," he writes. "The question is whether that opinion is of any value . . . Remember that while others can often point out problem areas, they rarely can give you good solutions."[42] Ultimately those solutions, have to come from us, one word at a time.

A Few Notes on Theses and Dissertations

When I arrived in Athens, Ohio, for my first semester of graduate school, I had big dreams about writing a book for my thesis. *I'm going to be writing anyway*, I thought, so *I might as well write a book*. Never mind that I didn't have a book-length story ready to share, let alone any idea of how to approach such a big project. I wanted to write a book, darn it! Books are sexy. Books make money. Books get you noticed!

Thankfully, it took only a few weeks of my first graduate workshop to realize that I still had plenty to learn about writing sentences before I could even think about the possibility of writing an entire book. That's not to say a graduate student never turns a thesis or dissertation into a book (Debra Monroe's first story collection *The Source of Trouble*, which won the Flannery O'Connor award, was Monroe's dissertation, unrevised, but that may be an exception that proves the rule). If a student shows up in my graduate program with a clear vision for a book project, I'm not going to get in their way. But for most students, completing several shorter projects will usually serve them better than putting all of their writing eggs in one book-length basket.

I tell students to think of graduate school as a training ground—a place to experiment and try new approaches, to get familiar with form, to become a master of the fine art of writing. Books will come, but start with the line, the phrase, the sentence, the image, the paragraph. Learn the basic footwork of a polished essay before attempting the acrobatics of a full-length memoir. Cut teeth on short story plots before hazarding the twists and turns of a novel. Write a one-act play before going for five. A sonnet before a sonnet sequence.

And for those hoping to compile a competitive writing portfolio (the kind that might help them get into a PhD program or land that first academic job), there are practical reasons to focus on shorter projects as well. Students who write several short stories, poems, or essays during their graduate program are more likely to complete at least one polished, publishable manuscript. And if we're submitting our best work to literary magazines, then in addition to banking a solid writing sample for future graduate school or job applications, we're also increasing our chances of getting published, which can add an extra competitive edge to those same applications. Contrast that with a student who spends all their time in graduate school working on a book. They may end up with a 200-page thesis, and some of that may work in excerpts as part of a writing portfolio, but the simple odds of getting one large manuscript published are much lower than if they've got several shorter pieces out there under consideration.

Even for students who decide to pursue a book-length project, not thinking of it as a book can still be helpful. "Defining my work as a 'thesis' protects the sprouts of inspiration and early drafts from falling victim to the trap of explanation," says MFA graduate Tabitha Blankenbiller. "Saying 'my book,' I've become convinced, is a curse. As soon as I've ever labeled a project book-worthy it falls apart."[43] Micah Cozzens, a graduate of my program, said that her thesis gave her "the unique luxury of writing something that doesn't have to go straight to market." This thesis mindset gave her more creative license to experiment and lean into the project as a tool for developing her writing skills—an opportunity "that the callous and fickle literary market seldom offers."[44]

The creative freedom of a thesis or dissertation is what makes graduate school so appealing to many writers—along with the structure and routine of classes, the motivation of course deadlines, and the time to explore one's writerly options. In addition to all that though, there are two elements of the thesis and dissertation process that are particularly useful and worth discussing in greater detail. The first is the thesis committee and the potential it offers not only for sustained professional critique but also for developing long-term mentoring relationships. The second is the reading list—a personalized bibliography of primary and secondary texts curated by the committee and designed to offer students the critical and creative framework necessary to complete their projects well. Choosing the right committee and building the right reading list can make completing a thesis or dissertation much easier.

Choosing a Committee

A thesis or dissertation committee typically consists of a committee chair and two readers. Students work closely with their chair to decide on a project, and the chair serves as the primary mentor during the writing and revision process. Readers typically come to the project as it takes final shape (though sometimes readers are involved earlier on), and they provide additional feedback and sometimes subject matter expertise. For instance, I once worked with a student writing about childhood trauma and her committee consisted of two creative writing professors and a trauma studies specialist. Another student whose thesis included modern-day fairytales had on her committee a short story writer, a YA novelist, and a folklore professor. An eclectic, expert committee can provide essential early reads to help us shape the direction of our project.

Perhaps more important than expertise though is personal fit. Tony Earley tells his students to prioritize the interpersonal dynamic. "Pick people you know, people you've studied with, people whose critical and aesthetic preferences you already understand," he says. "A thesis defense is stressful enough without some stranger showing up and going rogue on you."[45]

When seeking out committee members, we should be clear about what we want. Some professors are happy to offer regular feedback as the project progresses, while others may be more protective of their time until a first draft is closer to completion. In particular, if a professor enjoys some notoriety—if they travel for lots of visiting writer gigs, readings and interviews—they may have less time to offer a graduate student struggling with a batch of poems. And there are more practical issues to consider. Is the professor already mentoring so many other students that they may not have time for a new one? Will the professor be on leave during the semester we hope to defend our thesis? Are they about to retire? A friend of mine was two years into her PhD program in creative nonfiction when her committee chair—the only nonfiction writer on faculty—decided to retire. Without a mentor, her options were to transfer to another school or switch genres. Unforeseen interruptions and challenges are inevitable, but doing our homework before we assemble a committee can help us keep our energy where it should be—on the writing.

Compiling a Reading List

Most MFA and PhD programs ask students to compile and study a reading list that reflects their scholarly and creative interests. Some universities provide curated lists, while others leave the work entirely to students. All reading lists, though, are based on the same premise: thoughtful, informed students who know the critical, historical, and aesthetic context of their projects will always produce better work.

No student should treat a reading list as a perfunctory academic hoop to jump through. As Jennifer Emerson explains, a reading list can be "a roadmap of where you have been and where you are going as a writer." To Emerson, the list is "a declaration that you are open to growth and change" and a tool that "exists to expand your knowledge of both the craft and the business of writing."[46] A reading list is entirely personal, shaped by our interests, our aesthetic leanings, and our big questions. It serves as an independent course of study and an intimate conversation with authors and critics.

A thesis or dissertation advisor helps each graduate student create a custom reading list, and there are some general questions we can ask them to make that process more efficient: in the literary canon, which texts are most clearly in conversation with my project? Which texts serve as structural, aesthetic, or thematic models? Which scholars and critics are engaging with similar ideas? What texts and authors are out there that I don't know about yet? We're probably best off asking ourselves these questions first as we begin to create our own reading list and then taking our list and those questions to our committee. Then, the completed reading list serves as a customized reference guide, model text, sounding board, and source of inspiration. It becomes the idiosyncratic conversation we hope to join, and a yard stick for the progress we're making.

I REMEMBER JUST GETTING started in creative writing and wondering at what point I would truly deserve the title: *writer*. I was reading and writing a ton, but I had no audience beyond my classmates and no real sense that I knew what I was doing. Did simply writing make me a writer? Going to a dance club on the weekend wouldn't make me a dancer, I reasoned. And fixing dinner each night doesn't make me a chef. But what then separates the dabbler and the hobbyist from the real writer? Perhaps being able to say "I wrote today" is too basic a metric, but waiting to call ourselves writers until we've published something puts too much emphasis on external forces. I think we can call ourselves *writers* when we begin finishing what we start. Anyone can fill notebooks for days, but a writer puts in the work necessary to transform their furtive scribblings into art. A writer makes goals, commits to a routine, holds themselves accountable, and celebrates little victories. A writer trusts the process, works through writer's block, and seeks feedback along the way. We may or may not ever publish anything, but if we commit to the work of being a writer, that work will inevitably prove meaningful to us, and we'll have earned every right to bear the title.

7.

SUBMITTING WORK

I remember a few years ago receiving an email about an essay I'd sent to the *Southern Review*, a prestigious literary magazine that has been rejecting hopeful writers since the 1930s. For those who submit work consistently, such emails are as common as they are nerve-wracking, and they never cease to surprise, especially when they show up after so much waiting. An acceptance would mean validation for the months I'd spent writing, not to mention the privilege of sharing journal space with so many writers I admire, and some bragging rights among my friends. And there's the practical matter of money (the *Southern Review* actually pays its contributors). Then, of course, I opened the email and all that irrational optimism plunged deep into the pit of my stomach. "Dear Joey Franklin," the email began. "Thank you for sending us [your essay]. We enjoyed this piece, but we didn't feel it was right for the *Southern Review*."

Rejection is a sickening experience, something akin to airplane turbulence or bumping into your ex while they're out with a new fling. Neuroscientists have actually identified parallels between our response to rejection and our response to physical pain. And the more personal the rejection, the more pain we feel. Which is, perhaps, why writers often take rejection so badly, and why the fear of rejection so often leads us to procrastinate projects, put off revision, and ultimately fail to send out our best work to journals, editors, and agents.

Given the relatively low acceptance rates at presses and publications, submitting work might seem like a foolhardy endeavor, especially if our goal is fame and fortune (of course, if our goal is fame and fortune, then we're probably in the wrong business anyway). If, on the other hand, good writing is our goal, then submitting work can help us get there, and any publication, recognition (or money) that comes along the way can be a happy fringe benefit.

In the coming chapter, we'll discuss the value of making submission part of our writing process. Then, we'll introduce the nuts and bolts of submitting work to a variety of venues—from literary magazines and book publishers to multimedia venues and contests. Finally, we'll examine the potential promises and pitfalls of the self-publishing world and make a case that, despite what Amazon wants us all to believe, gatekeepers still matter.

Why Submit Now?

So many novice writers think of submitting work as what we do when we're finished with a project—a pie-in-the-sky step that maybe someday we'll get around to. But it's probably more helpful to think of submitting as part of the writing process—an essential step that helps us finish more work, see that work more objectively, and process rejection more productively. Sure it's a lot scarier to send out work than to keep it saved in files on our computer, but in the end submitting will make us all better writers, and it might even find us a reader or two.

Finish More Work

If your writing process is anything like mine, somewhere on your computer you've got a folder where you keep false starts, half-finished drafts, and nearly completed manuscripts that you don't know what to do with. If our only goal is to write, it doesn't much matter how full that folder gets. But if we want to participate in the literary conversation, to communicate with another person beyond our own friends and family, we have to find a way to move our manuscripts forward. By committing to submit our work, we create self-imposed deadlines that keep us in the chair and force us to not only complete drafts but to polish and refine them as well.

In compiling his essay collection *Partisans*, published in May 2017 by Black Lawrence Press, Joe Oestreich struggled to know whether his manuscript was really ready for submission. Then he got an email about an upcoming deadline for a book contest that gave him "a much-needed kick in the pants."[1] The contest motivated him to polish a few essays and plug a few thematic holes, and by the contest deadline he had a manuscript that finally felt complete. Oestreich didn't win that contest, but entering it helped him complete his manuscript and gave him the confidence he needed to keep submitting. Without the contest, he says, the book might still be sitting in a folder on his computer.

See Work More Objectively

Cultivating the ability to read our work objectively is crucial to our development as writers. And nothing helps cultivate that objective ear more quickly than revising a draft with a living, breathing reader in mind. Which is easier to do if we plan to submit to a living, breathing editor or agent. Near the end of her writing process, essayist Jericho Parms zooms in on the reader experience. "When I prepare to send work out, I always give it one final read with an eye to potential roadblocks I've created for a reader," says Parms. "Are my sentences clean and deliberate? Can my readers follow each trajectory I weave together? Where have I overindulged in language that might distance a reader who is new to my voice?"[2] For Parms, this self-interrogation is a key step in finding her unique voice in a manuscript—a voice that strikes a balance between her personal vision and the expectations of a potential reader.

Submission can also help us accept that we don't always know as much as we think we do about our own work. Nonfiction writer Matthew Gavin Frank thinks of submission as a way to give his writing some independence. He says he needs to "let it off leash . . . let it run around, allow other folks to have their way with it in order for me to really know what it is that I've done."[3] Frank's mindset can take some of the fear out of sharing our work with others. Instead of thinking of submission as a competition we hope to win, we can think of submission as an act of humility and community—perhaps an acknowledgment that writing has little hope of achieving its artistic potential if it is never exposed to the sometimes harsh light of the disinterested reader's eye.

Learn from Rejection

The novelist Anne Valente describes rejection as "one of the greatest teachers we have in our creative work." At its most basic level, rejection tells us that "one editor couldn't use our work,"[4] she says, but a series of rejections might be a good indication that a manuscript needs real help.

And a rejection might teach us other important lessons as well. For instance, rejection might be a lesson in selecting a more appropriate outlet for a manuscript. Rejection might be a lesson in the limits of experimentation or the strength of a particular voice or argument. Then again, rejection might just be a lesson in sticking to one's convictions. As Valente says, "Through years of writing and submitting, I think writers can hone their sense of what is good feedback and what needs to be revised, and what should remain."[5]

At the very least, rejection can help us cultivate thick skin and even a productive chip on our shoulder. "Feelings of rejection, if I'm lucky, turn into swagger," says poet Erica Dawson. "My poems are competitive with each other."[6] If Dawson submits three poems to a journal and two get accepted, she's "got to get that third poem to prove its worth," she says. In this imaginative way, Dawson transforms the negative emotional experience of rejection into the positive emotional experience of play. Rejection becomes a chance to revisit her work, listen to its voice, and judge it again on her own terms.

How to Submit

In the not too distant past, a writer had few options when it came to submitting work. Publishing houses for books. Community and regional theaters for scripts, and Hollywood production companies for screenplays. Magazines, newspapers, and radio for shorter stuff. Self-publishing has long been an option, of course, but it's often been considered an expensive, vain approach to putting work out into the world. For most of print history, publishing has been a small, exclusive club with powerful gatekeepers dictating what does and doesn't make it onto the page, stage, and screen.

Today those traditional venues still exist, as do many of those traditional gatekeepers. But technology (and the Internet in particular) has facilitated an explosion of digital media, creating unprecedented opportunities for writers to connect with an audience regardless of any gatekeeper. Write a novel and we might send it to an agent who may or may not agree to help us present it to an editor at some big New York publishing house. But we might also pitch it via book query to an independent or university press. We might post it on a public forum like Patreon, Substack or a personal blog. We might use Amazon's self-publishing service or serialize it as a podcast.

After writing several poems, we might submit them to literary magazines, but we might also post them directly to Instagram, produce spoken-word videos for YouTube, or print them in small batches on a letter-press to sell on Etsy. Similar opportunities exist for short stories, essays, memoirs, scripts and screenplays, and all manner of multimedia, experimental, genre- and form-bending writing projects. In the age of the Internet, whether or not we can find an audience for our writing seems predicated almost exclusively on our willingness to work.

But since each publishing route operates under its own unique aesthetic values, editorial standards, professional practices, and financial incentives, the work of submission will vary a great deal depending on what we're writing, where we're sending it, and how far along we are in our progress as writers. And though the Internet is replete with advice on how to submit our work, for many writers new to the publishing process it can be hard to know where to start. So I offer here a brief primer on how to submit various types of work, including an overview of the essentials and a nod to several reliable Internet resources for further reading (and also check out joeyfranklin.com/writershustle for even more resources).

Short Literary Work (Poems, Stories, Essays, etc.)

"If you write fiction, poetry, and/or creative nonfiction, you'll find that writing on spec is not only common; it's basically the rule,"[7] explains *Writer's Digest* editor Robert Lee Brewer. And by "on-spec," he means "on speculation." As in, now that we've written the dang thing, we hope someone will want to publish it. And this is true whether we're talking about poems in *The New Yorker* or short stories in a community college literary magazine. Sure some big name publications commission work from famous writers, but for the rest of us interested in traditional publishing, we have little choice but to toil away at whatever project we feel inspired to pursue and then hope some editor decides it's worth supporting. If we find that process discouraging, we might also find it reassuring, given that some of our most celebrated writers got their start writing on spec for small magazines. Anthony Doerr, Jesmyn Ward, Cheryl Strayed, Jericho Brown, Stephen King, and Alice Munro, to name a few.

And we might also take heart from the sheer number of publications that consider on-spec submissions. The community of Literary Magazines and Publishers (CLMP) has more than 600 members across the world.[8] Lyric poetry? Sci-fi short stories? Contemporary erotica? One-act comedies? There's a mag for that. Some have been around for decades, publishing some of the most famous writers in the world. Some just started yesterday and have never published anyone you've ever heard of. Some can afford to pay their writers, and some can barely afford their print runs. Each has its own, somewhat amorphous, artistic preferences tied loosely to the disposition and caprice of its (often volunteer) editorial staff. This means that as editors change, so too may a journal's aesthetic, especially since so many journals rely on a rotating staff of relatively inexperienced student readers for their initial screening process. Still, the best work usually makes its way to the top of the pile, which means that we can focus on making our work the best it can be and then put in the leg work to find the right venue for our manuscript.

Start by talking to professors, mentors, and other writers about where they send their work. Check out the back pages of anthologies such as the *Best American* series that publishes a bibliography of all their finalists, and look up the various literary magazine rankings available online. Those lists are hardly definitive, but they offer a good gauge of where excellent writing is being published. Also check out newpages.com, the most comprehensive database of literary magazines on the Internet. Most importantly, when we find journals that pique our interest, we should read some back issues to see if our work will be a good fit (check websites, the local library, or databases such as JSTOR or ProjectMuse), and maybe even consider subscribing (after all, if we want readers, we've gotta be readers). Most journals will post a mission statement that describes the kind of writing they're interested in, but typically these statements boil down to two basic principles: (1) a desire to publish the best writing the journal can find, and (2) a desire to promote voices that reflect and celebrate diversity.

Part of what we're doing in all this research is identifying target publications. But we're also learning how to make comparisons. Most literary magazines are okay with authors simultaneously submitting manuscripts to multiple publications, but it doesn't make much sense to send a poem to *The New Yorker* at the same time we send it to our local community newsletter. When I finish a manuscript, I send it out to five different venues at once— and I try to pick five places that I would be equally happy to publish in. That way if one magazine says yes, I don't feel bad about those other missed opportunities.

And though there's no standard stat-based ranking system in literary magazine publishing like there is in some other academic disciplines, we can divide them loosely into three tiers: At the top are the glossy, advertising-based magazines (*The New Yorker*, *The Atlantic*, and *Harper's*, for instance). At the bottom are small, upstart publications with only a few issues under their belt. Many are housed online and have yet to establish a reputation or a reader base. In the middle, we find the bulk of university-sponsored literary magazines (as well as some independent ones too): well-established publications with enough paying subscribers and/or sufficient institutional funding to support publication of a few issues a year. There are some standouts in this group (and they typically hold the top spots any time someone ranks literary magazines), but in general, any publication in this middle group is worth consideration.

After identifying a few target publications, check their specific submission guidelines and follow them exactly. If they set a word limit, we honor it. If they ask for anonymous submissions, we take our name off the manuscript. If they ask for a specific typeface or font-size, we deliver. If they want a cover letter, we keep it short and professional. And then we keep a record of where we've sent work so that if we do get an acceptance we can drop everything and contact all the other places we've submitted to and withdraw our manuscript from consideration.

The benefits of publishing in the lit mag market are relative artistic freedom and some modest exposure to a small but invested readership. The drawbacks? Few magazines can afford to pay their contributors, and those that do typically pay very little. There's also lots of competition. A typical literary magazine publishes only a small percentage of submissions (as low as 1 or 2 percent at some venues). On the one hand, this means that getting work into even a relatively unknown literary magazine can be tough. On the other hand, when we do land a publication we can take it as a fairly objective measure of our progress.

Articles for Commercial Publications (Freelancing)

While most literary magazines are labors of love subsidized by universities, arts institutions, or the goodwill and spare time of their editors, larger publications and presses often operate with less altruistic goals—they're in it for the money. These include national brands such as *Rolling Stone*, *Condé Nast Traveler*, and *Huff Post* as well as regional and trade publishers, and niche websites dependent on ad-based revenues. The success of these publications hinges on publishing content that lots of people want to read and then converting readers into cash, either by selling ad space, subscriptions, individual issues, or sometimes swag (T-shirts, coffee mugs, totes, etc.).

The trade-off in the commercial market is that while we have to produce content that editors think will sell, we're also likely to get paid for our work, either as a salaried member of the staff or as a freelance writer—an independent contractor paid per word or per article. And for those of us new to the game, freelancing is usually where we have to start.

The first step is to identify our field. Most freelance writers find themselves a niche topic to write about—their day jobs as a small business owners, their lives as parents, their adventures in travel, their experiences with hobbies like gardening or auto repair, or some aspect of their personal lives or identities. Even freelance journalists have a beat: politics, the economy, immigration, sports, film criticism, technology—it can be anything really, as long as we can either speak authoritatively on the subject or we know how to go out and get the story from those who can.

The next step is to identify publications related to our area of interest and learn their freelance policies. That may be as simple as looking at the publications we're already reading, but it also may require a little homework. For common interests such as parenting or politics, finding freelance venues might be fairly easy, but even publications covering more obscure interests can be found on Google without much trouble. In addition, Penguin Random House's annual *Writer's Market* includes not only an extensive list of publications that accept freelance work but also pages of expert advice on the practical aspects of freelancing.

Once we've identified our area of interest and related target publications, we have to find a story. The question to ask ourselves is the same question that editors ask every day: what do my potential readers care about? What do other small business owners, parents, travelers, or hobbyists need or want to know? What questions might they have that I could help answer? The first job of a freelance writer is to come up with a great story idea so that an editor doesn't have to. When we send in that idea, we want the editor to read it and think, "This is perfect for my publication."

Which brings us to how we present story ideas to editors. Most publications ask for a query letter (sometimes called a "pitch")—a short, detailed explanation of what the story is, why readers will care about it, and why we're the right person to tell it. Needless to say, in the commercial publishing industry a good pitch is invaluable (and later on in this chapter, we'll cover pitching in more detail).

Novels, Memoirs, and Book-length Nonfiction

The traditional publishing landscape for book-length creative projects can be divided into two categories: nonprofit publishing and commercial publishing. Where nonprofit presses rely heavily on institutional funding, grants, and endowments to keep their doors open, commercial publishers support themselves almost entirely on the sale of books. Which model we choose for our work will depend on a number of factors: At a commercial publisher, there will likely be more opportunities to make money in the form of advance payments and royalties, more of a budget for marketing, and, therefore, more potential access to readers. But often with all that opportunity comes both stiffer competition and an often-narrower aesthetic that is driven primarily by a book's presumed mass-marketability. At a nonprofit press, advances (lump-sum payments from a publisher at the signing of a contract) are often smaller (if they exist at all), as are marketing budgets. And as a result of those smaller marketing budgets, we generally have less potential access to readers. However, authors who publish at nonprofit presses generally retain more artistic control over their projects.

Depending on which approach we choose, we'll either work through a literary agent or directly with an acquisitions editor. Commercial presses rely almost exclusively on agents to help them find books to publish. Agents accept pitches from authors, and when they find a project they believe in, they agree to represent the author and their work. An agent then helps prepare and present a project proposal to various commercial publishers on behalf of the writer. And when a publisher buys a book, the agent will take a commission (usually about 15 percent) from what the author receives.

There are more than a few ways to find an agent. Look to authors writing similar work, and check their websites to see which agencies they use. Pick up a recent copy of Penguin's *Guide to Literary Agents*, checkout websites such as agentquery.com and querytracker.com. Talk to writing mentors, and look for agent features in trade magazines such as *Poets & Writers*, *Writer's Digest*, and *The Writer*. Each agent will have their own submission guidelines and preferred subjects and genres, so do a little research. And watch out for scammers. A real agent will never charge a reading fee, demand payment for editing services, or ask for money upfront.

At a nonprofit press, there's typically too little money exchanged in the contract process for an agent to get involved. Instead, an acquisitions editor accepts query letters directly from writers, and when the editor find a project they're interested in, they negotiate a publishing agreement directly with the writer. Later in this chapter we'll discuss how to pitch our work to both agents and acquisitions editors alike.

Poetry Collections

So far, much of the book publishing advice we have discussed won't be terribly helpful for poets. It's rare (unheard of, even) for a press to accept book proposals or pitches for a first-book collection of poetry. Instead, poetry publishers rely on a long-established system of contests to find and elevate the work of promising poets. There are more than one hundred such contests around the United States, and most operate in a similar way. Hopeful writers submit manuscript collections of poetry along with an entry fee. Those entries are screened by in-house readers, and then finalists are passed along to an external judge who selects a winner. Judges are often established poets with decent name recognition, and prizes typically include a modest cash award and publication.

Depending on who we ask, this system is either a shameless cash grab by underfunded presses that raises false hopes for the thousands of losing poets while promoting what one critic called a "consensus-by-committee" aesthetic that produces "vast parchments of conformity and mediocrity,"[9] or it's an egalitarian approach to publishing that invites developing poets to support the very art they propose to create and, as *Bellingham Review* editor Bailey Cunningham put it, provides "a place to stand on equal footing with submitters who have higher publication credits, and to connect your work with judges you admire."[10]

And yet, regardless of how one might feel about this system, for poets interested in traditional book publishing who lack an established relationship with a press (the kind that begins with publishing a first book), it is usually the best option. To learn more about the contests out there, consider the *Poets & Writers* magazine database at pw.org, or the members-only database at awpwriter.org. Also, talk to more established poets to get their take. And for an extensive bibliography of online resources to help organize and compose a poetry collection, check out the resources at joeyfranklin.com/writershustle.

Play Scripts

To produce even a one-act stage play can require an army of actors, directors, costume and set designers, lighting and sound specialists, make-up artists, and musicians—not to mention a venue, advertisers, and, of course, an audience to fill seats on opening night. But as most playwrights know, on the journey from finished manuscript to the dimmed house lights on that opening night there are many important steps along the way. And for playwrights just starting out, those steps often include contests, festivals, and open script calls. For the strongest submissions, these opportunities can lead to cash prizes, publication, staged readings, and even production. But plays can take years to polish, which means the most important ingredients in submitting play manuscripts are patience and endurance.

Contests and festivals: Most theaters will not accept complete manuscripts unless they come through an agent, so unestablished writers are almost always better off submitting their work first to contests and festivals, where new work by unknown writers often takes priority. "If you are just beginning as a playwright you don't need an agent," says playwright Christina Ham. Instead, she suggests we focus on "creating a body of work that will help you develop a name for yourself" and then "tirelessly submitting [that] work to contests and awards."[11]

Regional theaters and arts organizations sponsor hundreds of script contests and festivals large and small around the country. Some are "first play" contests, while others are aimed at students. Some are looking for local writers, and others home in on a specific demographic group. Two good places to start are the databases curated by the American Association of Community Theatre (aact.org/contests) and the Dramatists Guild (dramatistsguild.com), both of which feature extensive lists of contests, festivals, and other calls for submission, and provide a variety of resources for aspiring playwrights.

Open script calls: Many theaters will consider script submissions as long as authors work through established literary agents, and some theaters even allow inexperienced playwrights to submit script queries (a proposal that often includes a short synopsis of the play, a 10- to 15-page script sample, and a brief production history and author biography), but that doesn't mean playwrights should send out scripts and queries to every theater that will take them. Instead, take time to get to know the industry. "Join the playwriting groups on Facebook, LinkedIn, the Dramatists' Guild, and of course the Playwrights' Center," suggests Mary Sue Price. "Read theater magazines and blogs . . . Go to the theater as often as you possibly can."[12] Do some research on theater companies. What kind of shows do they typically run? Who are the playwrights they produce? Does the company have a specific mission or focus? How often do they invest in new work? As we learn more about the industry, we will identify theater companies that might be a good fit, and then we can start sending out our work.

Online resources: The Internet is home to a number of portals that connect playwrights, actors and other creatives with producers, directors, and theater companies. The most well known is the New Play Exchange (newplayexchange.org), which bills itself as "The world's largest digital library of scripts by living writers." Another is howlround.com, which for more than a decade has been a "free and open platform for theatremakers" that "amplifies progressive, disruptive ideas about the art form" and "facilitates connection between diverse practitioners." Given the democratic nature of such databases, the quality of work to be found can be uneven, but every year writers and producers make connections on these sites, and so these databases have become fixtures in the theater community.

Screenplays

In all writing fields, getting published requires a combination of talent, discipline, bravado, luck, and timing, but nowhere is that more true than in screenwriting. Partly because television and movie production requires so much time, money, and equipment (which screenwriters rarely have), and partly because so many writers are already in the game (two big screenwriters unions—the Writers Guild of America, East, and the Writers Guild of America, West—have combined membership of more than 15,000).[13] And yet, scripts good and bad get sold every day, and producers make them into TV shows and movies every year, so it's not an entirely futile effort to pursue screenwriting. The process is complex, though—more complex than can be covered fully here. Instead, consider this advice a starter kit for the aspiring screenwriter.

Get help: Script writing is almost always collaborative work. Whether from a professor, a beta-reader, a writing group, or a paid consultant, get other people involved. But if you do pay people for help, make sure they know what they're doing. As Garant and Lennon warn in *Writing Movies for Fun and Profit*, "A guy who talks about screenwriting but who's never sold a screenplay is not a "screenwriting guru," he's a "lecture circuit bullshit artist."[14]

Submit ~~good~~ great work: That may sound obvious, but screenwriting is a cutthroat business. "There are thousands of good scripts floating around Hollywood from writers already in the fold," writes Chris DeBlasio. "Those trying to break into the industry need to sell a top-notch product."[15]

Skip the agent (for now): The great paradox of screenwriting is that an agent can help drum up interest from producers, but most agents won't sign a screenwriter unless producers are already interested. Instead, says Jeanne Veillette Bowerman, if we're in the market for representation, "Approach managers . . . they're the ones whose jobs are most parallel to literary agents, namely honing your craft and career."[16] Resources such as backstage.com (a career platform for acting professionals), and sagaftra.org (an actors' labor organization website) offer helpful information about when and how to start looking for representation.

Query producers and managers directly: Many producers will accept unsolicited script queries. But, says Ken Miyamoto, "You have to do your homework . . . The worst thing that you can do is blanket send your query to all of the major production, management, and agency companies."[17] Instead, look for production companies that have experience with your genre of work, and research their preferred submission process.

Perfect your logline: Most managers, agents, and producers will want to see a logline as part of any pitch. A logline, as defined by Noam Kroll, is a "one or two sentence summary of your film that not only conveys your premise, but also gives the reader emotional insight into the story as a whole."[18] (For example, this logline for a famous Hitchcock film: "A wheelchair bound photographer spies on his neighbors from his apartment window and becomes convinced one of them has committed murder."[19] Can you name it?[20]). Loglines are a fast, potent way to pitch a script, but, says Kroll, they're also a useful writing tool.

Consider blcklst.com: Since 2013, The Black List (blcklst.com) has been a popular online forum for screenwriters to share scripts, receive feedback, and catch the attention of producers, agents, and managers. There's a moderate fee involved, but according to Black List success story Jason Hellerman, the site is "the best way for someone who does not work inside Hollywood to break into the industry."[21]

Look for contests: Winning a screenwriting prize can help an aspiring screenwriter garner some much-needed attention in an oversaturated market. But that all starts with submitting to the right kind of contest. The folks at Filmmarket Hub recommend submitting only to contests that offer "real rewards, no frills, and relevant opportunities."[22] This means that actual producers and agents are involved in the jury process and that the prize is established enough to actually produce that essential visibility. A few well-known contests include the PAGE International Screenwriting Awards, the Launch Pad Competitions, the Academy Nicholl Fellowships, the BlueCat Screenplay Competition, and the Scriptapalooza Script Writing competition, though there are many others.

New Media and Self-Publishing

Thanks to an explosion of Internet publishing platforms, it has never been faster or easier for storytellers, poets, journalists, and other creators to connect with an audience. There's the behemoth: Amazon's Kindle Direct Publishing, which has helped millions of people self-publish e-books.[23] But there are also crowdsourcing websites such as Kickstarter and GoFundme, and more recent paywall platforms such as Patreon, Substack, and Ghost are all carving out their own funding niches for business-minded creators. Add to that the thousands (maybe millions) of documentarians, podcasters, and vloggers producing work for platforms as diverse as Twitter, YouTube, Spotify, and the various social media platforms, and it all adds up to a brave new world of writing possibility.

Of course, fast, easy, and amateur are not always ideal ingredients in creative work, and just because we can self-publish doesn't mean we should. In fact, some of the very upsides that proponents of self-publishing champion can also be downsides. In the end, the question of whether or not to pursue any kind of self-publishing, online or otherwise, will depend on our appetite for entrepreneurial work and our stomach for selling not only our writing but also ourselves.

Consider first the most obvious advantage of self-publishing: no gatekeepers. A novelist needs no agent, no proposal, not even a copy editor. Anyone with a manuscript can get an e-book up on for sale on Amazon in as little as forty-eight hours. The same goes for the poet sharing verses on Instagram, the documentary filmmaker uploading videos to YouTube, the short story writer creating content on Patreon or the journalist writing a newsletter on Substack. Very little stands between a writer and their potential audience. And the success stories—Amazon self-publishers, YouTubers, independent journalists, and other storytellers with direct, unfiltered access to an audience that eats up their work and repays them with substantial ad revenue or paywall receipts—make this kind of self-publishing seem really attractive. One of the best-selling books of poetry in 2020 was written by a self-proclaimed "meditator, writer, and speaker" who got his start posting self-help poetry on Instagram.[24]

As potent as the promise of self-publishing seems, most who go this route aren't making a fortune let alone a living off their self-published work. And what we might gain in the immediacy of potential access we might lose in the sentence-level quality and intellectual depth of our work. "Gatekeepers are saving you from your own ego," writes Ros Barber, for *The Guardian:* "It can be frustrating, having your beloved book [or article, poem, documentary, or story] rejected by traditional publishers. But if you are serious about writing, you will simply raise your game."[25] For Barber and others like her, writing is an apprenticeship process, and bypassing gatekeepers also bypasses the many opportunities to improve our work that comes from critique and rejection.

Control is another oft-cited benefit of self-publishing. Novelists retain editorial control over every sentence but also over layout, cover design, and marketing. A citizen journalist will never face an editor telling them what news to cover and what to avoid. Poets on YouTube or Instagram can publish once a month or ten times a day, and they can set their verse on whatever gauzy background they choose.

But such control means that in addition to writing, there is a load of other work. As writing coach Tiffany Hawk explains, "To succeed at self-publishing, you will need to spend as much time and money producing, marketing, and managing your book/business as you spend writing."[26] And the ratio may be much worse than fifty-fifty. Some of the most successful self-published novelists on Amazon report working ten to twelve hours a day, with 90 percent of their time spent building their business and only about 10 percent on actual writing. For social media and pay-walled writers, it means creating a steady stream of content, networking, and drumming up subscribers. Lenny Rachitsky, who publishes a tech newsletter to a fanbase of 68,000 subscribers, describes the pressure as a boulder chasing him from week to week. "As soon as I put something out, I'm like, 'Okay, what's coming next week?'"[27] And though Rachitsky seems to like the pressure ("There's no better way to motivate myself to keep going and writing," he insists), it's a pressure that's built into the model. To self-publish successfully is to be an entrepreneur first and a writer second.

Another perk of self-publishing is the potential for direct access to an eager fan base of readers. This is particularly true for romance, fantasy, and other genres that have readers who often consume dozens of books a year and can be extremely loyal.[28] Take, for example, what happens on Kindle Unlimited, Amazon's e-book subscription service. Serious e-book fans pay a monthly fee for access to all those millions of titles (self-published and otherwise), and enough of them are willing to try out unknown, untested authors and then review and recommend their favorites. Amazon in turn promotes the most popular work on their website and in regular emails to their millions of users, all of which makes it possible for a self-published author to reach huge audiences—a feat that would otherwise be impossible without the herculean marketing effort of a major publisher.

But it's not just genre writers cashing in on the audience access that self-publishing offers. Over the past few years, writers of all kinds have started producing content for pay-walled platforms such as Patreon, Ghost, and Substack, in essence transforming themselves into small media companies. Many of these writers (including big name journalists, bloggers, fiction writers, and web comic illustrators, among others) have turned to these platforms as a way to transform massive social media followings into paying audiences. They offer newsletters, short stories, video chats, private forums, and other member-only content in an intimate, personalized setting, and in exchange, readers pay a subscription fee. The most successful have amassed tens of thousands of subscribers and raise thousands of dollars a month in direct income from their audiences.

But online popularity is fickle, difficult to cultivate and hard to maintain. Many (but by no means all) of the best-selling novelists who've gone the self-publishing route were already successful writers with traditional presses. The same goes for many writers who've cultivated followings on social

SUBMITTING WORK

AN ETHICAL GUIDE

"A WORD ONCE SENT ABROAD CAN NEVER RETURN."
~ HORACE

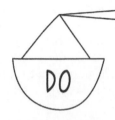

GET TO KNOW THE MARKET
› ASK MENTORS FOR VENUE SUGGESTIONS
› READ THE VENUES YOU WANT TO PUBLISH IN
› RESEARCH AGENTS OF YOUR FAVORITE AUTHORS
› CHECK OUT THE WRITER'S MARKET

GET SOME SKIN IN THE GAME
› SUBSCRIBE TO LIT MAGS
› PAY (REASONABLE) SUBMISSION FEES
› BUY BOOKS FROM INDEPENDENT PRESSES

SUBMIT TRULY FINISHED WORK
› WRITE YOUR GUTS OUT
› GET FEEDBACK
› REVISE, AND REVISE AGAIN

MANAGE YOUR SUBMISSIONS RESPONSIBLY
› KNOW WHAT & WHERE YOU'VE SUBMITTED
› TRACK SIMULTANEOUS SUBMISSIONS
› WHEN A PIECE IS ACCEPTED, WITHDRAW IT ELSEWHERE

SEND OUT UNFINISHED WORK
› (DON'T MAKE MORE WORK FOR EDITORS AND AGENTS UNTIL THAT WORK IS WORTH READING)

FOCUS TOO MUCH ON PRESTIGE
› (THERE'S MORE THAN RANDOM HOUSE & THE NEW YORKER. LIT MAGS & INDIE PRESSES ARE A GREAT PLACE FOR GOOD WRITING)

PAY TO PLAY
› (MOST NON-PROFIT LIT MAGS & CONTESTS CHARGE MODEST FEES, BUT BEWARE OF AGENTS & 'CONSULTANTS' WHO CHARGE $$$)

TAKE REJECTION PERSONALLY
› (LASHING OUT AT AN EDITOR MAY FEEL GOOD, BUT THEY HAVE FEELINGS TOO, AND MEMORIES. DON'T BURN BRIDGES BY BEING A BAD LOSER)

FIGURE 7 *"Submitting Work: An Ethical Guide," with an epigraph from Horace, "Ars Poetica," Perseus Digital Library, March 1, 2022, http://www.perseus.tufts.edu/ hopper/text?doc=urn:cts:latinLit:phi0893.phi006.perseus-eng1:347-390.*

media or pay-walled platforms. They first developed name recognition in traditional media outlets and then ported over all those readers to a pay-walled service. It's much easier to capitalize on an audience that already exists in the form of readers and social media followers than to try and build readership from scratch.

I don't say all this to discourage anyone from pursuing self-publishing on the Internet or otherwise, but to paint a clear picture of the pros and cons. Self-publishing can absolutely be a helpful (and even financially viable) part of any writing life, but the work involved in producing and marketing our own material and in developing an online persona to help expand our reach may risk turning the art and craft of writing into just another job.

For the undeterred, though, there are some ways to make the most of self-publishing, whether we're uploading slam poetry to YouTube, putting a novel up on Amazon, producing our own podcast or simply keeping a semi-public blog of personal thoughts on life.

Try Traditional Publishing First

"Do not consider self-publishing until you have spent at least a few years working on your writing, making submissions, and learning about the business of publishing,"[29] suggests Harold Underdown. And though "a few years" may be too long for some to wait, the sentiment is worth considering. Time spent writing for gatekeepers "won't be wasted time," says Underdown. "Even if you don't get published, if you do decide to self-publish later you will be much better equipped to do so successfully."

Find a Niche

Part of self-publishing is finding our tribe online and then writing to it. CNET's David Carnoy writes, "Nonfiction books with a well-defined topic and a nice hook to them can do well, especially if they have a target audience that you can focus on."[30] This is as true of religious texts and technical manuals as it is of self-help books and genre fiction. When we self-publish, our target audience is not traditional book critics or industry experts but peer members of our particular online communities—communities that can be both fiercely devoted to our work and forgiving of our writerly shortcomings, especially if we're offering content those readers will value.

Love What You Do

So much of the self-publishing discussion revolves around self-promotion and developing an online persona. Ros Barber actually says, "If you self-publish your book, you are not going to be writing for a living. You are going to be marketing for a living."[31] But most writers don't pursue writing because they love marketing. They put up with marketing because they love writing. Whether we're talking about YouTube, Substack, or Instagram, and whether we're writing a blog or a novel, we better make sure we love the content enough to put up with the rest of the work. Patreon founder Jack Conte suggests looking for the "overlap" between our passions and what will "resonate with [our] audience."[32] He cautions against producing content to simply please the crowd. "It has to be a real thing that you yourself love. Otherwise, it's too hard to be a creator. You'll give up."

Pitching

We may spend years of our lives completing a project, but the question of whether or not we find readers will likely depend on a few carefully chosen sentences written well after a project's done.

This is true for commercial publishing, nonprofit publishing, and self-publishing. We've got to get good at making a case for our work, whether that happens face to face with agents and editors at a conference, in a one-paragraph email pitch, in a longer query letter, in a full book proposal, or even through writing content for our own book jacket, podcast description, or online ad.

The One-Sentence Summary

If we're working on a book or other larger project, we should have a one-sentence answer to the question "What's it about?" The one-sentence summary of a novel should introduce the plot ("*Life of Pi* is about an orphan who survives months at sea in a lifeboat with a tiger named Richard Parker"), while the one-sentence summary of a poetry collection might focus more on theme ("Jericho Brown's *The Tradition* examines the growing presence of terror and trauma in our lives—and introduces a new poetic form called 'the duplex'"[33]). In both examples, the summary introduces the project's main themes and tensions while enticing readers to learn more.

The Short Query Letter

These formal pitches can be as short as a single sentence in an email or as long as a multipage letter, but all good query letters include the same basic elements:

- The hook: an engaging introduction to the project
- The specifics: a brief summary of the project's details
- The rationale: a discussion of why the project matters and what makes us the right person for the job

Note, for instance, the telling details in Belcamino opening hook to a query letter pitching a mystery novel:

Dear [Agent],

I am seeking representation for my crime fiction novel, BLESSED ARE THE DEAD. This novel was inspired by a story I covered as a crime reporter and my own efforts to get a serial killer to confess to taking and killing a little girl.[34]

Here, Belcamino offers intriguing personal information that simultaneously hints at her novel's plot and how she'll approach it—like a gumshoe journalist who'll do anything to get her story.

Every pitch needs an engaging introduction, but it must be followed by at least a paragraph or two of equally captivating specifics. Even if the project isn't a murder mystery but, rather, an article on, say, at-home gyms, these few paragraphs must articulate not only what the project is all about but why somebody would want to read it and why we're the person to write it.

Consider the main paragraph from Alex Christian's successful pitch to *Men's Fitness* magazine for an article titled "Home Comforts" about the rise of digital home gym workouts. After describing the proliferation of workout apps, streaming workout services, and digital fitness equipment, Christian poses the article's main question: "Can gadgets and remote workouts really replace the gym?" Then he lays out the article in detail: "I'll be exploring how technology is reshaping the fitness industry, and asking PTs [physical trainers], industry experts and the bright minds behind leading fitness tech brands about the future of exercise."[35]

The meaty specificity of this paragraph shows Christian's depth of knowledge and his ability to write a sentence. All that makes it much easier for an editor to say "yes," when they get to the end of a pitch.

The final argument in any query letter should be about why we're the right person for a particular project. Let's look at the last paragraph in Georgia Perry's successful pitch to *The Atlantic*, for an article titled "Mall Walkers: The Suburban Exercisers Keeping America Wholesome." Early in the query letter, Perry establishes her general writing credentials by mentioning other places that have published her work (CityLabs, *Portland Monthly*, and *Vice*), but in the final paragraph she drives home why she in particular is prepared to write about mall walking:

I spent last summer in Minneapolis and, knowing I wanted to write about mall walking in some capacity at some point, spent a morning walking with the official Mall of America walkers ("Mall Stars"). I also interviewed the mall's PR person, Tara Niebeling, who was really cheery and vocal about how much the mall "loves our Mall Stars."[36]

Here she highlights her personal experience and her commitment to the project. *Look at the work I've already done*, says the query. *Boots on the ground observations. Notes. Interviews.* And Perry leaves the reader knowing that she's ready to do more.

> I'd love to pull on this experience, as well as some more research . . . to give readers a deeper understanding of mall walking and its quasi-subversive origins. I think to many people mall walking is just a "weird, funny thing old ladies do," but there's a lot more to it than that. These old ladies are challenging the Capitalist system and winning![37]

A successful query letter makes an editor's job easier by introducing not only a good idea but also a good writer. "People are time-stretched," says Alex Christian. "You want the commissioning editor to read that pitch and immediately go, 'Great idea, done.'" So, says Christian, "You should get really straight to the point and justify every. single. word."

The Book Proposal

If we think of a query letter like speed dating, then a book proposal is like a forty-eight-hour first date combined with an FBI background check and a medical exam. A good query letter may pique an editor's interest, but, at least in the case of nonfiction books, the editor is likely going to ask for a lengthy proposal.

And while each publisher establishes its own guidelines, in general a proposal includes an introduction, a chapter-by-chapter synopsis, a defense of the book's commercial viability, and a presentation of the author's credentials. It's a chance to show off our prose styling but also our depth of thinking and our preparation.

So how to go about writing a proposal? Model texts can help (several of which I've archived at joeyfranklin.com/writershustle), and so can hot tips from publishing professionals. Here are just a few:

Know your audience: Future Tense Press founder Kevin Sampsell tells me, "the most common mistake writers make is taking the carpet bomb approach to submitting . . . Whenever I get submissions for fantasy books, thrillers, kids' books, or self-help, I know the writer has given little effort in getting to know what Future Tense is about. In the end, it's a waste of my time and the writer's time."[38]

Keep in mind the bottom line: "Rather than thinking of your proposal as an introduction to the book, think of it as a business case for why it's worth a publisher's time and investment,"[39] writes Kristin Wong for the *New York Times*.

Write as if the book is already finished: "A proposal can be an exercise in sleight of hand," says Erika Goldman of Bellevue Literary Press. "It should appear that you've already written the book and have the table of contents determined when you may not yet have written more than an introduction or a couple of chapters."[40]

Focus on what makes you different: Microcosm Press reminds submitters, "We have heard every hollow and meaningless line in a book pitch. We want you to think about your proposal and deliver something that is uniquely your own after looking at everything that is out there. (Spoiler alert: There are a LOT of books out there)."[41]

Pay attention to practicalities: Bloomsbury Academic reminds authors to "cover all the practicalities," including "the likely word count, inclusion of images or copyright material, your proposed delivery date and whether there are any digital or mixed media considerations to be aware of." (In my initial proposal for this book, I failed to account for images and had to renegotiate with the press to include the infographics and illustrations).

Negotiating

There are entire books written on the subject of how to negotiate publishing contracts, not to mention countless articles (and I've listed several good ones at joeyfranklin.com/writershustle), but there is one principle to remember: everything is negotiable. Advance payments. Royalties. Cover design. Gratis copies. Author discounts. Everything.

When our work gets accepted for publication, be it a poem, a story, or a book, the publisher will provide us with a contract to sign. Read it carefully, and make note of the rights it grants but also what rights it may take away. Do we retain creative freedom? Does the copyright remain ours after publication? Is there an advance payment? What are the royalty percentages on sales? Does the contract say anything about republication rights or movie rights? Short or long, contracts are legally binding, and we should know what we're being asked to sign.

Then, before we sign, we should get some help. It can be hard to know what points of a contract are industry standards and what are signs that a publisher is playing hardball (or trying to take advantage of an inexperienced writer). A mentor can help parse the details and can offer counsel about what to accept, how to negotiate, and occasionally, when to walk away. It's also not a bad idea to consult a lawyer, especially if the contract involves a substantial amount of money.

I'VE BEEN SUBMITTING WORK for nearly two decades, and I collect rejections like some people collect love letters. I print out the emails and keep them in a green file folder in my desk at work, and I like to show them to students—not out of some form of self-flagellation but as a reminder to them and to myself that submission and rejection are part of the process of becoming a writer. If we aren't submitting, we aren't taking advantage of the most effective tool writers have for turning rough drafts into final drafts. If we aren't submitting, we aren't engaging in an important step in finding our own voice on the page. And if we aren't submitting, we're missing out on opportunities to discover where our work fits in the grand public conversation.

And yet, is publication essential? Maybe not. Ultimately, as a writer I'm interested in language and stories and in translating the mess of my own heart and mind onto the page. Publication is secondary. If I were a plumber or an accountant, I would still write. From a personal perspective, I don't need the validation of an agent, editor, or some other gatekeeper. However, to think of the author/gatekeeper relationship as only a professional matter or as merely a necessary evil in the otherwise idyllic life of the writer-artist is to shortchange the role of a disinterested reader in the creation of literary art. By committing to make submission part of our writing process, we acknowledge that writing, at its most valuable, is a private act with a public end. And in that way, our commitment to submitting work can become a commitment not only to the writing life but also to our community.

8.

CONSIDERING (MORE) SCHOOL

Way back in 1983, when the exponential growth of university creative writing programs had only just begun, Donald Hall stood at a rostrum at the Association of Writing Programs Conference at New England College and wondered aloud whether we shouldn't "abolish the MFA."[1] He compared university creative writing programs to sweatshops, fast-food kitchens, and automobile assembly lines. He described their workshops as "institutionalized cafes" where homework assignments reduce creative work to "parlor games" that "trivialize and make safe-seeming the real terrors of real art." The industrialization of creative writing was, as Hall saw it, ruining American letters, shifting our focus from pleasing "the muse" to pleasing our peers, and creating an insular community of "academic" writers often wholly disconnected from the American reader.

What might Donald Hall say today about the more than 300 graduate creative writing programs in the United States? The 700 undergraduate programs? The tens of thousands of degree-holding "writers" who leave school without a clear vocational path (and what might he say about a book like this, aimed at professionalizing those writers?)? Certainly if we're thinking about applying to one of these creative writing programs (undergraduate or graduate), we would do well to heed Hall's skepticism, and ask the question, *Do I really need a creative writing degree?*

For those hoping to teach creative writing at the university level, the answer is yes—an MFA is necessary, maybe even a PhD. But for everyone else, the academic route may not be ideal. Compared to many educational paths, creative writing offers little in terms of straightforward direction toward gainful employment. Instead, what it offers is the opportunity to invest in ourselves as writers. It offers time to read widely and deeply; space to hone our skills in storytelling, persuasion, and creativity; and the opportunity to develop an authentic voice. It offers the support of experienced mentors and committed peers. It offers lessons in giving and receiving criticism, and it offers a chance to participate in a larger literary community.

It would be a mistake, though, to think of creative writing programs as merely artistic retreats removed from all practical considerations. Yes, a good creative writing program helps us think, write, and live more like the writers we want to be, but it also offers many of the benefits of a traditional liberal arts education—an enhanced capacity for critical thinking, communication, creativity, and analysis as well as concrete skills in teaching, editing, and project management. And as is true for any liberal arts student, a creative writer's vocational success depends almost entirely on our willingness to hustle.

In short, except for those interested in the obvious (and decidedly more narrow, uncertain, and highly competitive) academic job track, no one *needs* a formal creative writing education. However, if a person needs to write, a creative writing program can be an excellent place to do it, especially if that person has the will to create their own opportunities, and the stomach for a little uncertainty. For that writer, I offer here a brief overview of the various creative writing degrees, along with some advice on finding the right school and putting together a successful application.

Undergraduate Programs

The Association of Writers and Writing Programs database[2] lists more than 700 colleges and universities that offer at least an undergraduate minor or concentration in creative writing, while roughly 300 offer a bachelor of arts (BA) degree and 34 offer a bachelor of fine arts (BFA). And while these programs vary in size, funding, course offerings, and extra-curricular opportunities for students, it's probably most accurate to view these not as highly specialized programs of artistic training but as part of the broader tradition of the American liberal arts education. Students in these programs typically study the fundamentals of creative writing in tandem with literary analysis and criticism and alongside a core of general education requirements. And as with other liberal arts programs, creative writing helps students develop a broad set of skills that will be useful in a variety of career paths. It also offers excellent preparation for graduate studies in creative writing, though a writing-specific undergraduate degree is rarely a prerequisite for creative writing graduate work, nor is it necessarily preferred. Let's look briefly at the different undergraduate paths for creative writing.

English major concentrations: At some colleges and universities, students who major in English can concentrate their studies (hence the name "concentration") around creative writing. This usually means a student will complete a set of general courses common to all English majors and also enroll in a series of coordinated courses specific to creative writing.

Bachelor of arts or bachelor of fine arts: Some institutions go a step further than the English major concentration by offering a BA or BFA in creative writing. Often the difference between these degree tracks is nominal, with each typically requiring a balance of coursework in both creative writing and literary studies. However, some BA and BFA programs in creative writing include more workshop courses, some publishing or editing curriculum, and in BFA programs in particular, a thesis or senior project component. Some programs are open enrollment while others require an application.

Creative writing minor: A supplemental course of study in creative writing that is separate from a student's major. Typically between one and two semesters of credit, a minor often includes foundational classes in literary studies augmented by beginning, intermediate, and advanced coursework in creative writing. Some minor programs allow students to emphasize a particular genre, while others require cross-genre study. In addition, many programs require a capstone project or an internship.

Certificate and other non-degree programs: In time commitment and scope, certificate programs are similar to creative writing minors but are designed for students who have completed their undergraduate studies and are not yet interested in or ready to apply to graduate programs. In fact, many certificate programs frame themselves as a half-step between undergraduate and graduate work, allowing students to develop a writing portfolio and build relationships with potential recommenders—two important parts of the graduate school application.

Graduate Programs

Graduate degrees in creative writing are offered at the master's and doctoral level and provide students specialized training in the craft and theory of creative writing as well as coursework in literary studies with an emphasis on preparing students to teach in a university setting. However, at least at the master's level, it's still useful to think of creative writing as a highly specialized liberal arts field that prepares students broadly for the professional world. And while all graduate degrees offer focused time to write, access to mentors, a built-in writing community, professional training, and the motivation of external deadlines, each prioritizes different aspects of the academic creative writing life. Here's a breakdown.

Master of Fine Arts: The sexiest of the creative writing degrees, a master of fine arts offers students two or three years of advanced study in the craft and theory of creative writing, usually with a genre focus in areas such as poetry, fiction, creative nonfiction, genre writing, writing for children, screenwriting, playwriting, and literary translation. I say *sexiest* because despite the proliferation of MFA programs in the United States, despite the uneven quality of the education from program to program, and despite the seemingly abysmal job prospects for MFA graduates (more on that in the next chapter), the degree still holds a certain social and intellectual cachet that just isn't there with an "ordinary" master of arts degree in English or even a PhD. *Real writers earn an MFA*, or so the reputation suggests. Of course, that's a heap of nonsense, and we'll talk more about that, but first let's parse out what distinguishes an MFA from other graduate degrees in creative writing.

As with the BA and BFA, the MFA is broadly a liberal arts education but with a more intense curricular focus on the craft, theory, and (sometimes) business of creative writing. The degree culminates in the completion of an MFA thesis—an original creative work of (ideally) publishable quality that a student must present at a formal defense. An MFA thesis typically begins with a critical examination of the student's work as it relates to the broader literary tradition and is followed by forty to eighty pages or more of creative work, depending on specific program requirements.

Most MFA programs are designated as either "full residency," in which students attend class in person each semester and participate in campus life, or "low residency," in which students take online or correspondence courses and come to campus for just a few weeks each year. Full-residency programs typically offer students tuition reimbursements and stipends in exchange for teaching freshman composition or introductory creative writing courses. Low-residency programs, on the other hand, offer few funding opportunities and typically charge higher tuition than their full-residency counterparts. What makes low-residency programs attractive, though, is flexibility. Because low-residency students can take courses from anywhere in the world, they don't have to quit a job or relocate to a new city in order to study.

Beyond residency distinctions, all MFA programs fit into one of two subcategories: the studio MFA or the academic MFA.

- **The studio MFA:** A program dedicated entirely to creative writing. Students enroll in workshops and (often) craft and theory courses but are not required to complete literature seminars or other traditional academic coursework. The Studio MFA is most attractive to those students who want to focus primarily on their writing, and not other aspects of the academic life. Studio MFA students may or may not have teaching opportunities.

- **The academic MFA:** Like the BFA in creative writing, the academic MFA requires students to enroll in not only creative writing workshops and craft and theory courses but also in more traditional literary studies courses. This dual approach is ideal for MFA students with an interest in working in the academy and possibly pursuing a PhD. Academic MFA students will almost always have teaching opportunities.

Master of arts: A master's degree in English is traditionally considered a stepping stone toward a PhD (though as with the BA in English, plenty of students who earn an MA then go on to use those skills in other fields). MA coursework includes seminars in literary analysis, critical theory, research methods, pedagogy, and other subjects that prepare students for the rigors of a doctoral program. Within some master's programs, students may choose an emphasis in creative writing. These programs still require the traditional core of academic courses of a standard literary studies MA but give students the option to take several creative writing courses and to complete a creative thesis. And while earning an MA may not carry the prestige of an MFA (nor grant the terminal degree that qualifies a graduate to teach university creative writing), there are a number of reasons to consider both types of degrees when looking for a graduate program in creative writing.

- First, any worthwhile MA program with an emphasis in creative writing will offer the same opportunities as an academic MFA: workshop courses; teaching, research, and editorial internships; visiting writer programs; travel funding and other professional development perks.

- Second, MA programs are often easier to get into than MFA programs. Not because standards are lower but because competition isn't nearly as stiff. A well-established MFA program may receive hundreds of applications each year, while a comparable but less well-known MA program may receive just a few dozen. Because there are fewer applicants vying for spots at an MA program, acceptance rates are often much higher than MFA programs.

- Third, MA programs are almost always two-year ventures, while many MFA programs require a three-year commitment. Completing a degree in two years can mean less debt and quicker access to the job market.

- Finally, for students planning on doctoral work, the traditional academic course requirements of an MA can be invaluable— not just in terms of scholarly preparation but also in terms of actual doctoral credits. Often PhD programs will allow students to count some of their scholarly MA course credit toward their doctoral course requirements which can, in turn, shorten the time to complete a doctoral degree by as much as a semester or two.

Doctor of philosophy (PhD): The doctorate is reserved for students who have demonstrated mastery of a particular field and who are prepared to offer significant, scholarly, professional, or creative contributions to that field and to teach others along the way.

When we talk about a doctoral degree in creative writing, we're almost always talking about a doctoral degree in English with a specialization in creative writing (at least in the United States). Like the MA in English with a creative writing emphasis, this doctoral degree allows students to focus on creative writing through coursework and a creative dissertation while they also complete the same scholarly coursework required of traditional doctoral students.

A doctoral program in creative writing helps students develop expertise in the craft and theory of a particular genre and also expertise in that genre's literary, cultural, historical, and aesthetic context. In addition, most doctoral programs require students to select a secondary scholarly specialization (something like a doctoral minor), and to complete pedagogical training through coursework and teaching assistantships. Successful doctoral candidates qualify themselves to teach creative writing at the university level but often also qualify themselves as a generalists, capable of teaching a broad range of subjects in literary studies.

Students accomplish all this in four phases: coursework, comprehensive exams, the dissertation, and the dissertation defense.

- Coursework: Students begin with roughly four semesters of coursework—a mix of literature seminars, creative writing workshops, and supplementary courses in critical theory, pedagogy, and research methods.

- Qualifying exams: Once coursework is completed, students take a qualifying exam that evaluates their expertise in their given specializations. Exam questions are drawn from a reading list compiled by each student in coordination with advisory faculty (the dissertation committee). This reading list consists of specialization-specific primary and secondary texts, and students often dedicate several months to reading and exam preparation. The exam itself often takes the form of a series of essay questions prepared by the dissertation committee, and while students have traditionally been expected to take the hours-long exam alone in an empty room on campus without notes or Internet, doing their best to cite sources from memory, many programs have moved to a take-home format wherein the student is given a weekend to prepare more polished (and more thoroughly cited) responses.

- Dissertation: Upon successful completion of the qualifying exam, a student earns "doctoral candidate" status and must complete a significant creative project in their genre of specialization (often 100–200 pages in length) along with a critical introduction that examines the literary, cultural, historical, and/or aesthetic relevance of the project.

- Defense: The final step of the process is a public defense of the dissertation before the dissertation committee. The candidate will field questions from the committee about the form and content of the creative work as well as questions about how the project fits into its broader literary context and how their doctoral studies have prepared them for professional academic life.

In addition to all this scholarly and creative preparation, most doctoral programs offer pedagogy courses and hands-on teacher training to help prepare students for careers as instructors at colleges and universities. Alongside their own coursework, students typically teach one to two classes per semester in freshman composition or other entry-level undergraduate subjects.

Who Needs a PhD?

I think it is safe to say that no one should pursue a PhD in creative writing unless they are dead set on teaching at a college or university. And even then, we should be really certain that the extensive academic training, literature seminars, pedagogy classes, and other academic demands are actually what we want in our writing life. If all we're looking for is time to write, a doctoral program is not the answer.

However, if we're determined to pursue a university teaching position, then we have to consider a PhD. Yes, the MFA is a terminal degree, but we should think of it as the minimum requirement. In addition to MFA, hiring committees are looking for significant teaching experience, significant publications, and the ability to teach more than one subject—whether that's other creative writing genres or other disciplines such as literature, journalism, cultural studies, or rhetoric and composition. Earning a PhD doesn't guarantee us a leg up on the academic job market, but it does give us more time to rack up the accomplishments and gain the experiences that ultimately will.

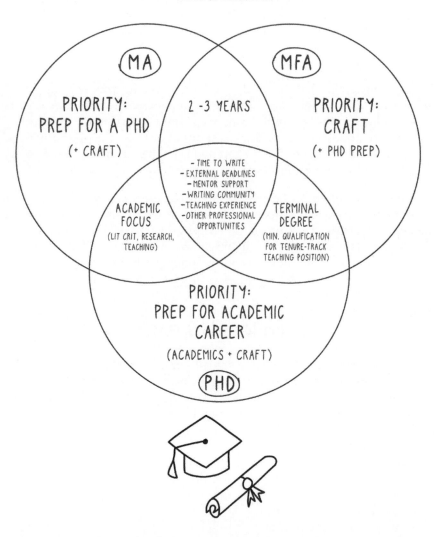

GRAD SCHOOL

WHICH DEGREE IS RIGHT FOR ME?

"IT IS NOT ENOUGH THAT OUR EDUCATION DOES NOT SPOIL US:
IT MUST MOREOVER, ALTER US FOR THE BETTER."
– MICHEL DE MONTAIGNE

MA

MFA

PRIORITY:
PREP FOR A PHD
(+ CRAFT)

2 - 3 YEARS

PRIORITY:
CRAFT
(+ PHD PREP)

- TIME TO WRITE
- EXTERNAL DEADLINES
- MENTOR SUPPORT
- WRITING COMMUNITY
- TEACHING EXPERIENCE
- OTHER PROFESSIONAL
OPPORTUNITIES

ACADEMIC
FOCUS
(LIT CRIT, RESEARCH,
TEACHING)

TERMINAL
DEGREE
(MIN. QUALIFICATION
FOR TENURE-TRACK
TEACHING POSITION)

PRIORITY:
PREP FOR ACADEMIC
CAREER
(ACADEMICS + CRAFT)

PHD

FIGURE 8 *"Grad School: Which Degree Is Right for Me?" with an epigraph from Michel de Montaigne, "On Pedantry," Essays of Michel De Montaigne, Project Gutenberg, March 1, 2022, https://www.gutenberg.org/files/3600/3600-h/3600-h. htm.*

How to Choose the Right Program

Success in any creative writing program requires a base level of talent—some natural curiosity, some fitness with the sentence, an eye for image, and an ear for rhythm. But as James Baldwin reminds us, "Talent is insignificant . . . Beyond talent lie all the usual words: discipline, love, luck, but, most of all, endurance."[3] Whether we're talking about a creative writing minor, a doctoral degree, or anything in between, the best programs will not only foster our natural talents but also provide opportunities to apply the discipline, love, luck, and endurance that Baldwin says is so important.

In practical terms, this means looking at every aspect of a program, from faculty and funding to coursework and extra-curricular activities. And the keyword is *opportunity*: what opportunities do we want or need at this stage of our writing career, and how might a particular program provide them? Of course, everyone's needs will be different, but here are few baseline questions to consider.

Location: Do I need to stay local for work, family or other obligations, or could I move across the country for the right program? Where might I be comfortable living? Big city? Small town? The desert? The coast? Do I need a vibrant nightlife? Good schools for the kids? Great restaurants or the great outdoors? Am I okay outside my cultural comfort zone? What kind of rent can I afford? On the one hand moving for school can mean a real disruption to life. On the other hand, a few years in a less-than-ideal city may be worth it for the right program.

Funding: Does the program offer scholarships, financial aid, stipends or other monetary support, and if so, how much? Are all students funded or is there competition for only a few fellowships or assistantships? Is there funding for research, travel, or professional conferences? No one short of James Franco[4] should enroll in a creative writing program that doesn't offer at least partial funding. And no one should take out a big student loan to get a creative writing degree. The job prospects are just too fickle to consider anything but the most modest debt in order to pay for school.

Thankfully, most reputable programs offer teaching assistantships wherein a graduate student receives a tuition waiver and an annual stipend in exchange for teaching one or two undergraduate classes per semester. At the most well-funded programs, students can choose to work as teachers, research assistants, assistant editors, assistant program administrators, and in other professional positions.

Faculty: Who are the writers on staff? Are any of them retiring soon? And are they a diverse enough group that I'll likely find a mentor who can support my work from both an aesthetic and a sociocultural perspective? What are their publication records like, and more important, what's their reputation for working with students? Just because a writer has published several books and garnered a little fame doesn't mean they know how to teach. Talk to current and former students about which faculty to seek out (and maybe which to avoid).

Coursework: How many workshops will a program offer? Is that enough to help me meet my writing goals? What about literature seminars or theory classes? What else in the course catalog might be interesting? Do the course offerings focus heavily on the traditional western canon, or do they also explore diverse voices and subjects? How will the curriculum challenge me and expand my understanding of the literary tradition? How will the curriculum prepare me to meet my future writing goals? To enter the job market? To apply to future graduate school? To build other skills? Elective coursework in editing, publishing, project management, and teaching can help us prepare for an academic career as well as other professional opportunities.

Professionalization: What kind of professional preparation does the program offer? If it's a graduate program that offers students teaching positions, are there also research assistantships or other campus positions? What about editorial positions at literary magazines or campus publications? Other internships? Community initiatives? Study abroad? Does the program offer career services such as practice interviews, dossier services, job fairs or an alumni-mentoring network? With few exceptions, a program's reputation alone won't open many doors. Instead, it's the actual professional preparation a program offers that will make the difference after graduation.

Extracurriculars: What's the culture of the program? Is there a healthy sense of community? Do faculty make time out of class to get to know their students? Do students feel like colleagues in a cooperative or like contestants in a competition? Are there readings, open-mic nights, holiday parties, or other social events? No matter how great the coursework is, if a creative writing program doesn't help students cultivate a sense of community, it can be a very lonely place.

Rankings: Does a program ranking matter? I hate to even bring up the topic because measuring reputation is such fuzzy business, but Google will provide rankings if we go looking, so it's worth a few notes. In short, ignore program rankings. Rankings can offer a general overview of how various programs compare to one another, but no generic set of metrics will compare to our personalized ones. Only when we've looked at a program's curriculum, researched its faculty, spoken with current students, and then considered all the other community, demographic, regional, and cultural factors unrelated to the school itself can we really make an informed decision about whether a program is right for us.

Better to conduct our own research and create our own rankings by placing all the answers to our questions in a spreadsheet. Place school names in rows along the far left of the sheet, and then order questions in columns across the top, starting with the most important questions first (those will be different for everyone). Then as we gather information about various programs, we drop our answers into the spreadsheet. With all that information in one place, comparisons are quick, and narrowing down our options can be fairly painless.

How many schools we apply to will depend on our budget for application fees (which can range from $35 to $90 each). My most promising students typically take a swing at three or four really competitive programs, three or four other attractive programs they discovered in their research, and a few schools close to home that meet their criteria. I'm not sure there's such a thing as a "safety school" in creative writing—there are so many great writers in the country, and every program has a competitive application process—but as we do our research, we'll get a feel for which programs seem realistically within our grasp and which ones feel like long shots.

Applying to Graduate School

Every program has its own application requirements, deadlines, and procedures, and getting those wrong can end an application process before it even starts, so be sure to double and triple check the protocols for each school. In general though, an application will include academic transcripts, letters of recommendation, a personal statement, a writing sample, a resume or CV, and maybe a score from the GRE (the General Records Examination, a standardized test that's meant to predict a student's likelihood of success in graduate school). The most important component of the application is the writing sample, followed by the personal statement and letters of recommendation (though not necessarily in that order). Everything else merely signals to the committee (and the school) that we've got the general academic competence to make it through the program.

The writing sample: I think it's safe to say that no one has ever gotten into a creative writing program based on the strength of a GPA, GRE test score, personal statement, or letter of recommendation. All of that can help a strong writer stand out in a crowd, but no stellar academic record can make up for a weak writing sample. On the other hand, a strong writing sample might be enough to get us into a program, even if our academic record is less than competitive. It should showcase our talents at the sentence level and our understanding of the basic elements of genre, but it should also give reviewers a sense of our curiosity, our creativity, and our depth of thinking. "I want to see that applicants have taken care with their samples, and that they have a sense of what is being published today," writes Kendall Dunkelberg. "I don't really care a lot about what style you write in, at least not initially. I'm mostly looking for care with language, feeling for form, and attention to detail."[5]

The personal statement: Here's our chance to introduce the admissions committee to the person behind the writing sample. A committee will want to know why we hope to study creative writing, but they're ultimately looking for evidence that we'll be a good fit in their program. They want to see that we're humble and teachable but confident enough to have plans for the future. They want to know who we're reading and what we're doing now to invest in our own literary community. What they don't want? An anecdote about our lifelong love of literature or a humble brag about the ten novels we wrote in high school.

Some suggest using a personal statement to explain anomalies in an academic record—a failed class, a low GPA, a semester of withdrawals. But, says Cady Vishniac, "it's impossible to bring this up in a way that doesn't come across as excuse making, or serve to draw attention to a problem the [committee] might not have even noticed or cared about before."[6] Vishniac's a fan of asking recommenders to address any academic issues in their letters. The right professor can offer context for any problems on a transcript, and, says Vishniac, they can reassure the committee "that I'm actually a responsible person" that can be "trusted to stick with the degree."

Letters of recommendation: Because this is one part of the application that we don't write, it might seem out of our hands, but we can control quite a bit about what goes into these letters. First, as Tom Provost says, "make sure you know the professor and that the professor likes your work. This may seem obvious but I am often surprised by people who come to me for requests, people whose work in my class was substandard or people I don't really know at all."[7] If a recommender can't speak glowingly about our work, we shouldn't put them in the tough spot of having to either decline the request or write a lukewarm letter. Second, we can guide the kinds of things a recommender writes about. "Give folks the information you want them to highlight and pay attention to," says Kisha Lewellyn Schlegel. "Did you win an award or write a novel last year? Have you taught writing in the schools? What genre will you focus on and why?"[8] The right recommender will be enthusiastic about our application, but they can ground that enthusiasm in specifics only if we provide them the necessary details.

Finally, every writing professor has been asked for a letter of recommendation a few days before the deadline, and most professors end up writing them because they know the stress of applying for graduate schools, jobs, and scholarships. But when a professor sits down to write a letter, do we really want them thinking about how disorganized and unprepared we are? Sometimes last-minute asks are unavoidable, but in general we have a professional obligation to respect a mentor's time and make our request well in advance.

Curriculum vitae (CV): An academic CV differs from a resume in that a resume briefly highlights various skills and accomplishments tailored to a particular job while an academic CV generally includes a complete record of our education, publications, presentations, teaching experience, service positions, and awards. Most CVs are fairly thin at the beginning stages of a writing career, so don't worry too much about its length. The goal is to list completely and honestly all relevant professional activity.

And while there's no set typeface or layout for a CV, we should aim for readability and clarity. Use a clean font and be consistent with the hierarchy of headings and the use of white space. The most important rule, though, is honesty. As we list our teaching experience, publications, awards, and other accomplishments, we should avoid exaggeration or misrepresentation, and only include accomplishments that are relevant to an academic career. Finally, a CV is a living document, so whatever format we decide on should be easy to edit and add to as our careers progress (see several examples at joeyfranklin.com/writershustle).

Comparing Offers

Best-case scenario when we apply to creative writing programs? We get multiple offers. In that situation, we might pull out those questions we answered during our research and start the comparison process over again. Look at faculty, at funding, at community. Look at professional development and teaching opportunities. Decide which program offers most of what we want, and make sure to compare apples to apples. For instance, one school may offer more funding, but it might be in Boston or New York where the cost of living could be prohibitive. One school may host several public readings a year but offer little by way of student interaction with visiting writers, while another school may host fewer visiting writers, but offer in-depth master classes with each.

If we haven't yet talked directly with faculty or students, now is the time. Advice from our own professors and mentors can be helpful too, especially if they have relationships with faculty at the schools we're considering. Finally, consult family members and partners. Most graduate schools will notify students of their acceptance in late February and will give applicants until April 15 to make a final decision, so take some time to mull it over. Then take a breath, and make the choice.

Handling Rejection

The hard truth of applying to creative writing programs, especially graduate programs, is that most applications get rejected. It may be that our writing sample was not strong enough to make the final cut. It may be that our creative interests weren't a good fit for the department. When those rejections start to come in (and they surely will), resist the urge to take them personally. Don't, for instance, write an angry letter to the program director (or a whiny one, a defensive one, or a passive aggressive one that says something like, "Well, I guess your school's not interested in original writers"). Do ask for advice on how one might improve an application. Do talk with trusted professors and mentors for their counsel, and then take all that counsel to heart and consider applying again the following year.

LET'S END THIS CHAPTER on the question we started with. Does anyone really need a degree in creative writing? The answer comes down to what we mean by *need*. Do we need a degree to call ourselves writers? Of course not. All we need, according to Alexander Chee, is work ethic and "a wiley, cagey heart in the face of extremity, failure, and success."[9] But he continues, "if you cannot endure, if you cannot learn to work, and to work against your own worst tendencies and prejudices, and you cannot take the criticism of strangers, or the uncertainty, then you will not become a writer." For Chee, it was an MFA program where he learned all those things. So no, we don't need a degree—but it can help.

And what about need, as in *I need some money*? It can be tempting to think of education in terms of simple dollars and cents. There are easier, less challenging, less heartbreaking, less maddening ways to make a living, but there's something to be said for the need to pursue our passions. The value of a creative writing education cannot be measured "in a straight, utilitarian line between a degree and a profession" says Amsterdam University College professor Huan Hsu. Sure, creative writing offers training in soft skills that will be widely applicable in a variety of professional settings (and we'll spend the whole next chapter on that very subject), but what it offers is much more than a liberal arts track into middle management. "Maybe I'm being old-fashioned or high-minded," says Hsu, "but I think there is only an upside to pursuing an education in your interests. The world would be a better place if there were MFA graduates everywhere. If there were MFA graduates in congress, working for non-profits, working at banks."[10] And perhaps that's true because at its most pure, the pursuit of creative writing isn't merely about critical thinking, communication skills, or even art, but about shedding light on what it means to be human. And in the end, isn't that the education all of us really need?

9.

PREPARING FOR A (WRITING) CAREER

Years ago when I was researching graduate programs in creative writing, mulling over whether or not I should even apply to one, I came across two articles that have stuck with me. The first was a note by novelist Charles Everit Poverman published on the website of the MFA program at the University of Arizona. Poverman described the MFA as little more than "a temporary haven and situation in which your work can be taken seriously." Then he painted a bleak picture of a creative writer's sobering career prospects in which the impossibility of finding a steady academic job forces the smarting writer to "turn to secondary interests," "seek more marketable degrees," or simply "retrain themselves" by going "into law, psychology or whatever else interests—and supports—them."[1]

The second article was "Teaching Creative Writing" by Russell Celyn Jones, and one line has lingered like a playground insult. "No one," writes Jones, "should get a Ph.D. in creative writing unless it's a racing certainty that he'll also be nominated for a Nobel Prize."[2]

Such skepticism of creative writing as an academic discipline was old news twenty years ago but is still expressed today, if not by well-established writers,[3] disgruntled professors,[4] or disillusioned students,[5] then by STEM-minded parents who can't understand why the potential of their bright, ambitious child is being dashed against the rocks of something as impractical as creative writing.

Of course such skepticism hinges on an outdated, narrow, and largely false notion of the professional possibilities of a creative writing education. It's absolutely true that most creative writing students won't publish creative work, won't go on to academic jobs, and (perhaps most discouragingly) won't even keep up a personal writing life, but those facts are almost immaterial to the question of whether or not a creative writing education can help prepare students for rich, successful professional lives.

As with other liberal arts degrees, it may be more accurate to think of creative writing less as a path to a specific career (though it can be, and we'll talk about that) and more as a path to a variety of professional fields. A writing education will teach us how to compose a pleasing sentence, how to organize a narrative, develop a character, and mold a metaphor, but it offers so much more than that. Creative writers are creative thinkers—we're trained to listen, to read what's going on beneath the surface, to ask questions, offer critique and process feedback; we're trained to imagine other worlds and other possibilities and to anticipate the needs of strangers. Revision—the willingness to improve and progress—are built into our psyches, and we've cultivated a sense of communication as both an art and a craft.

Throw a stick in any direction and we hit a professional industry that needs the talents of creative writers. We may see ourselves as poets, fiction writers, essayists, or playwrights, but we should also see ourselves as master communicators and problem solvers with valuable skills that can be uniquely adapted to any number of professional situations. And though we may have initially gravitated toward the liberal arts because we couldn't imagine life on some gritty business or entrepreneurial track, it is just that kind of hustle—that disciplined willingness to lay our own path forward—that helps creative writing students leverage our education into all manner of meaningful, satisfying work.

Creative Writing Skills in the Real World

Consider the following examples from three creative writing students who leveraged their educational experience into unique, fulfilling professional lives. Take special note of how each student let their interests and strengths guide them and how they put themselves in situations that lead to more opportunities.

Mila Myles: Political Communications Specialist

Mila Myles credits Aaron Sorkin's TV drama *The West Wing* for inspiring her career as a political communications specialist. In college, Myles was a creative writing major with a minor in history. She enjoyed writing, but she couldn't see herself holed up all day working on a novel, and her real passion was politics. "I started bingeing *The West Wing* in my junior year, and for the first time I realized that speech writing was a job."

Myles stayed in the creative writing major but narrowed her focus to creative nonfiction. She added a political science minor and then applied to a study abroad in international journalism. She calls this her "speech writing triangle," a custom educational scaffolding that helped her complete two master's degrees in global communications and then work as a digital media coordinator, communications director, and campaign spokesperson for political candidates across the country.

"What's powerful about being a creative major," says Myles, "is that you are not successful unless you are challenging the norms and trying to innovate." Creative writing taught her critical and creative thinking skills that she uses every day. "It's part of my being," she says. "Every time I need to solve a problem, I'm now more attuned to look for creative solutions, for the paths less traveled."

"Most people think [a creative writing degree] is a waste of money," she continues. "And it absolutely can be if you don't think it through." But, she explains, if we combine our love of writing with our other professional interests and then use that multidisciplinary vision to guide our choices, we can prepare ourselves for just about anything.[6]

Nick Gray: University Safety and Security Director

When Nick Gray started college, he thought he wanted to be an engineer. "I think I had bought into this very American mindset that you get an education for something very specific and very technical that's going to make you gobs of money," he tells me. But after a semester, he decided engineering wasn't a good fit. "I could have done it," he says, "but I would have gotten out of there with a wreck of a GPA."

Gray ultimately chose creative writing because it played to his strengths. He describes himself as a kid who "burned through books like nothing," who grew into an adult "obsessed with books and narratives that could trigger an emotional response." He enjoyed his classes, especially the emphasis on conversation, debate, and the challenge of developing a convincing argument, but creative writing was never a career goal. "I always knew that I wanted to do something else primarily, and maybe keep writing as a hobby," says Gray, so he tried to stay open to possibilities.

One day on a whim he attended a law enforcement recruitment lunch on campus. "I was bored, and they had free food," he says. "And I'd never met an FBI agent, so I decided to go." Gray watched students gather around the agents from the FBI, DEA, and ATF, but back in the corner were "two little short blond ladies" from the Postal Inspection Service. "I remember thinking, *these ladies drove all the way out here, and nobody's interested in what they have to say.*" So Gray did the nice thing, struck up a conversation with the two women, and ended up leaving with a phone number for the postal inspector in Gray's home town of Philadelphia, Pennsylvania. A few days later, he called the inspector and by the end of the conversation had lined up an internship.

"I spent the summer confiscating kilos of cocaine out of the mail and helping kick in doors and arrest drug smugglers," explains Gray. "It was awesome." But it wasn't just the action that made the job great. "The investigations required a lot of thinking and processing and predicting human behavior. There was a lot of planning and a lot of collaboration." He spent half his time in the office and half out in the field, and that, he discovered, was exactly the kind of career he wanted.

After graduation, he applied to a sheriff's department in Lafayette, Indiana, and started work as a deputy, where he was surprised to see his creative writing experience come in handy. He used his critical reading and analysis skills to understand and interpret the law and his communication and argumentation skills when interacting with the public. "Those things came in so, so clutch out on the street, dealing with people that are potentially having the worst days of their life," says Gray. Today, he works as the director of safety and security at Wabash College in Crawfordsville, Indiana, and those same creative writing skills are proving just as useful.

"My job is very broad," explains Gray. "Sometimes it feels limitless." Being responsible for ensuring the safety of an entire campus community means a lot of teaching, conflict resolution, negotiation, and explanation. It means convincing a lot of different stakeholders to accept policies that they may not like. "The ability to deliver that message without pissing people off is critical," says Gray, and he gives a lot of credit to his creative writing education. His ability to get to the root of an issue, to understand different perspectives, and to talk someone through something difficult all started at school. "The basis was really in the classroom—talking about [difficult subjects] with your friends, your colleagues, and your peers—defending your point . . . I didn't even realize these were skills that I had until I got out there in the real world."[7]

Khara House, Director of Community Engagement

Khara House excelled as an English major at Northern Arizona University. She loved both writing and teaching, and on the advice of a professor she pursued a master of fine arts in poetry. "My initial intention was to teach," says House, and after she completed her MFA, she worked as a university instructor for eighteen months. But "with not much room for advancement, a middling salary in a high-priced town, and no guarantee of contract renewal," she started preparing to move back home to Pennsylvania. Then one day a leasing agent at her apartment complex mentioned that her company was hiring and that House might be a good fit if she wanted to stay in Arizona. "Long story short, within a month I was hired; after a day,

I was offered the assistant manager position, and after about a year and a half, I became the community manager."

Today, House works as the Director of Community Engagement, a job that combines her creative energy with an interest in local housing policy. In addition to writing legal reviews, public relations content, and marketing copy, she writes grant proposals, gives presentations to legislators at the local, state, and national level, and she recently helped develop a strategic plan for the historic Black community of Flagstaff, Arizona. "Ultimately who I am as a writer has formed who I am as a masquerading professional," she tells me. "My work may be corporate, but the soul of it still beats with a poet's heart." Not that her work calls for much poetry but that her daily writing projects demand the same set of creative skills she learned as a student. And, says House, "I still feel that thrill that comes when the perfect turn of phrase spills out onto the page."

House certainly appreciates her liberal arts degree, but she wants students to know what they're getting into: "I started my undergraduate studies in 2004, when it was still the rage to say 'You can do anything with a Liberal Arts degree!'" In her experience, though, that has only held true for students who were willing to imagine themselves in a variety of positions and then embrace opportunities as they come. "Finding a career that allows you to be creative requires creativity in the pursuit," says House. And perhaps a little bit of putting ourselves in the right places so we can be there at the right time. "If any word describes my career path post-graduation, it really is *serendipity*."[8]

These three examples highlight a few essential ingredients in finding satisfying professional work as a creative writer. Note how these writers focused less on checking boxes as they marched toward some predetermined career goal and more on learning who they really were and how they wanted to spend their days. Then they put themselves in situations that helped them do just that. Following our passions doesn't mean we have to starve, but it does mean that we have to remain flexible and expand our notion of how we can apply our passions in new ways.

Preparing Now for Professional Life

"If you want to succeed in life," writes Fareed Zakaria in his book *In Defense of Liberal Education*, "most often you need to put in the hours, develop good habits, work well with others, and get lucky."[9] That is, in short, what these three writers and others like them have managed to do. They've worked hard, remained curious, pursued their creative interests, and learned how to translate their skills in a way that employers understand. And yes, luck has something to do with it. But successful people create their own luck as often as they stumble across it. They seek out new experiences, say yes to a wide range of opportunities, and prepare themselves to embrace the next right path as it presents itself.

I say "next right path" because, as Zakaria goes on to explain, the twenty-first-century economy is constantly evolving, and no matter what we study, it will likely prove "somewhat irrelevant to the day-to-day work you will do soon after you graduate."[10] Today's students are less likely to build a career with one employer than they are to build a set of professional skills that they use with a variety of employers. "What remain constant are the skills you acquire and the methods you learn to approach problems," writes Zakaria. And, "given how quickly industries and professions are evolving these days, you will need to apply these skills to new challenges all the time."

As students of creative writing, our ability to find a happy, productive, fulfilling professional life will depend in large measure on our ability to remain patient amid such uncertainty and change and at the same time keep ourselves on the lookout for new ways of applying our skills. In practical terms, this means cultivating experience through real-world scenarios that help develop some out-of-classroom confidence as creative, critical thinkers. At my university we call this "Humanities+," as in take your humanities education and add something to it—professional competence refined in the laboratory of practical application. And there are so many practical applications. Here are just a few.

Creative Writing+

If we're enrolled in a creative writing program, we ought to think about other coursework that can augment our workshops and seminars. Perhaps there's another field we're interested in that might complement our degree—marketing, digital humanities, computer programming, editing, graphic design, or even business. Think of our earlier example of Mila Myles and how she prepared for future work by combining creative writing classes with political science. We might take a targeted class or two or enroll in a minor program. In doing so, we exercise our creative skills in new ways, expose ourselves to broader professional possibilities, and cultivate the kind of versatility that employers find attractive. It's not just about doing creative writing and some other subject, but about channeling your creative writing skills through that other subject.

Internships

Perhaps the most direct way a creative writing student can prepare for professional life is by completing an internship (or two, or more). Research suggests that internships are more important than just about anything for helping students find that first job after graduation.[11] The reason, writes University of Michigan's Gina Shereda and Joseph Stanhope Cialdella, is simple: in an internship, students learn skills directly from industry professionals and have daily opportunities to "demonstrate [their] ability to work collaboratively for an organization and illustrate [their] commitment to a particular type of work."[12] Internships offer a low-stakes professional environment in which creative writers can put their soft skills to work and gain some clarity about what they have to offer the professional world. Internships also help students develop relationships and connections that can come in handy when it's time to go on the job market.

Employment

My first year and a half of college, I worked as a campus custodian cleaning toilets in the early hours of the morning. The job paid well and left me plenty of time to study. Eventually, though, I figured I needed some professional experience that would prepare me for life after college. I found two part-time campus jobs that put my English major skills to good use—writing public relations copy for the school of education and working as a writing tutor. I spent my days bouncing from class to the PR office to tutoring sessions and back to class again. The experience gave me my first taste of a professional identity, and I discovered that I really enjoyed writing and teaching. Any work in college is a good idea, but professional work serves us the way an internship does—it gives us practice applying our education in new ways and helps us discover what our interests are and where our skills lie.

Volunteer Work

Many worthy organizations would cease to exist without the help of volunteer labor. And many of those volunteer positions offer the same kind of professional development as internships or paid positions. Within our own writing communities, there are likely arts centers, libraries, schools, prisons, literary magazines, and other organizations that would be thrilled to have our help. And volunteering has the added benefit of getting us out of the college bubble. In my freshman year I spent a semester teaching literacy at the local prison. I didn't have any profound *Stand and Deliver* moments, but one prisoner's penchant for inappropriate tangents did teach me some important classroom management skills. In the right position, we can put our interests and passions to work and do something good for the community and ourselves at the same time.

Teaching and Research Assistantships

Many colleges and universities offer teaching and research assistantships for both undergraduate and graduate students. These students work alongside professors teaching courses, evaluating student work, conducting research, or assisting in other projects. Students get to observe the professorial life up close and get a feel for what it's like to spend all day teaching and researching. And there's no better way to build a relationship with a professor who may later serve as a professional reference. Many research positions also expose us to interests and disciplines that we may not have pursued on our own. Kath Richards, the illustrator for this book, started out as my research assistant helping conduct interviews and editing drafts, but in a brainstorming session on book design she agreed to try her hand at illustration, which led not only to her designing the infographics and icons for each chapter but the book cover as well.

Study Abroad Programs

There are many ways to study in another country, and some are more conducive to professional preparation than others. There are study abroad programs that serve more or less as extended vacations, but others offer challenging coursework and real-world experiences that help students develop into global citizens. "Our trips abroad need to intersect with our local lives," writes Anu Taranath. She argues that "interacting with people across difference while we are abroad, however well-intentioned we might be, does not make any of us a global citizen unless we are willing to rethink who we interact with at home and how."[13] In other words, the ideal study abroad would be one that marries our creative and intellectual passions with the global issues that matter to us most. Then it's up to us to apply our skills in a way that prepares us to be better citizens when we return home.

If we go about any one of these activities in the wrong spirit, we might reduce them to little more than soulless resume padding. But when we approach them intentionally, with the aim to strengthen our skills and discover new professional possibilities, they constitute an essential component of the liberal arts education—one that helps creative writers recognize the intrinsic value of their skills and cultivate the confidence necessary to find a place for those skills in the world of work.

Pursuing an Academic Career

All this talk of expanding the value of one's liberal arts education is fine, but what about those who are hell-bent on becoming creative writing professors? I certainly was, and I can't fault someone for sharing the same goal. But it would be unethical to pretend that academic creative writing is a growth market. The fact is that most MFA and PhD graduates won't go on to full-time, tenure-track positions at some college or university. "There is no sustainable career path in academia for MFA holders in creative writing," wrote John Warner back in 2014. "Do not think you're the exception to these realities," he warned. "You are not."[14] And while Warner didn't explicitly mention PhD graduates in this article, the situation is more or less the same. The problem, continues Warner, is that "each year, we graduate thousands of newly minted degree holders and there are very, very few career-type teaching jobs to absorb them."

Those who do land one of these coveted positions will already have a significant publishing record, robust teaching credentials, and other ample professional experience that help catch the attention of search committees. That kind of portfolio can take years to compile, and in the meantime, less-qualified graduates have little choice but to keep trying to publish while they fill part-time teaching gigs for low pay and no healthcare or retirement benefits. After a few hiring cycles, if they haven't published well enough to make them competitive in the full-time, tenure-track market, many decide to move on to more stable and more lucrative work, often outside the academy (which is one reason for the entire first half of this chapter).

And yet as bleak as the situation is, there are positions that need filling. Professors move. Or they retire. Or they quit and go on to other things. Occasionally, new creative writing programs are created or old ones expand, and in that way, positions open up for creative writing faculty. There's nothing wrong with pursuing one of those positions as long as we take certain concrete steps now to make ourselves as competitive as possible and then embrace the improbability of an academic career by preparing seriously for a professional plan B.

Qualifying for the Job Market

Academic careers are built on scholarship, teaching, and citizenship. Scholarship (or in other words, publishing) will almost always be the most important marker of professional success in the academy, particularly while on the job market. Even universities with no publishing expectation for their faculty will often look more favorably on an applicant who is publishing than one who is not. A close second to publishing is the ability to teach, and closely behind that is citizenship—our ability and willingness to serve in the department, the school, and the larger academic community. In all situations, search committees are on the hunt for "trajectory"—evidence that we are already on the path to doing the kind of work that they need done. Academic hopefuls should start immediately to cultivate experience in each of these three areas and then prepare to articulate them in an application and during an interview.

Publishing: What kind of publishing record are search committees looking for? A few common adjectives: Active. Significant. Strong. Distinguished. Excellent. Successful. This might mean a recently published book with a nationally recognized press or several short stories, essays, or poems in well-respected literary journals. "Peer reviewed, or refereed, journal articles are the gold standard,"[15] writes Karen Kelsky, author of *The Professor Is In*. For creative writing, this means manuscripts accepted for publication by disinterested readers at publications with solid reputations. It definitely doesn't mean *one random piece published in a venue no one's ever heard of*, or *three book reviews*, or *a half-dozen conference presentations*.

Preparing for the job market means polishing manuscripts, getting feedback from readers, talking with mentors about where to submit work, and then sending out our best stuff as soon as it's ready. It also means making rejection part of the writing process—revising manuscripts when they get turned down and sending them out again soon. For novelists or memoirists, it means producing shorter work alongside our larger projects—essays and short stories that we can use to build our publishing portfolio now. We may ultimately want to write book-length projects, but if we don't also produce shorter work, we increase the risk that we'll have no publications in our portfolio when the time comes to apply for jobs.

Teaching: To most search committees, quality teaching matters as much as publishing. Phong Nguyen, director of creative writing at the University of Missouri, recommends students get as much teaching experience as they can in creative writing and in literature and composition as well. He also suggests enrolling in pedagogy courses and considering a certificate in college teaching. "You have to show that you care about teaching," says Nyugen. "It's essential to stand out."[16] Search committees will be looking for creative approaches to instruction and learning, an awareness of current pedagogical practices and a commitment to diversity and inclusion.

Citizenship: In addition to writing and teaching, faculty do a lot of professional service. They advise students, sit on thesis committees, serve on faculty senate, perform peer reviews, edit journals, and organize conferences. And all departments need leadership—committee chairs, department chairs, ombuds, and communications officers. So volunteer where it's needed. Organize student activities, plan a reading series, read submissions for a journal—find a way to contribute. "Colleges and universities are run in a model of shared governance," writes Natasha Sajé. "Your future colleagues— who will be hiring you—want to know that you're the kind of person who volunteers for work."[17]

Preparing Applications Materials

A search committee will typically request a letter of application, curriculum vitae (CV), writing sample, and letters of recommendation. They may also ask for philosophy statements on teaching and diversity, and they might even request copies of student evaluations from previous courses. In the following section, we'll discuss how to tailor the various parts of an application to fit the unique needs of each school we're applying to. (And for more resources, including sample documents and links to all kinds of good advice on the nitty-gritty of applying to faculty positions, visit the resources pages at joeyfranklin.com/writershustle.)

Letter of application: The purpose of this letter, writes Victoria Reyes, "is to introduce who you are as a scholar, what you would bring to the department as a potential colleague and how you fit the requirements listed in the advertisement."[18] Reyes warns against cliches, jargon, and hyperbole and says that the best letters are built on concrete evidence—our publishing record, our experience, and our awards or honors. "Fact-based statements that highlight your accomplishments show, rather than tell, the reader of your commitment."

For a specialized creative writing position (one for a fiction writer or poet, for instance), this letter can highlight our expertise in a specific genre—how our scholarship, teaching, and citizenship inform one another and how we see ourselves contributing to the larger academic discussion in our field. For generalist positions (where the search committee is looking for someone who can teach composition and literature in addition to creative writing), we're better off focusing on our breadth of experience and expressing enthusiasm for working as a team player. English departments value such a spirit of cooperation and volunteerism, especially if the department is small, understaffed, or underfunded.

Writing sample: Reviewers are looking for a compelling example of our work—something that highlights our fitness with language, our depth of thinking, our cultural awareness, and our relationship with tradition. But they're also comparing us to other candidates. So while our writing sample should give readers a clear picture of our aesthetic ability, it should also hint at what we might bring to the classroom and to the larger academic conversation.

For specialized job postings, our sample should highlight our expertise in a particular genre—demonstrating our awareness of tradition and our confidence in contributing to it. For generalist or multi-genre positions, we might consider a multi-genre writing sample, especially if we've published work in more than one genre. But even if we haven't published in multiple genres, we can use the application letter to make a case for how our writing, teaching, and citizenship experience has helped us develop the expertise necessary to teach more than one genre.

Letters of recommendation: In addition to measuring the quality of our academic records, search committees are charged with determining whether or not we will be a good fit in the department. Letters of recommendation help committee members contextualize our academic work and cultivate a sense of how we are viewed by those who know us best. And while a single glowing recommendation can be written off as bias or hyperbole, consensus among reviewers can be persuasive.

Who we request recommendations from will depend on the jobs we are applying to. For instance, if the job includes helping run a student magazine and we've worked at a magazine, a recommendation from the editor might be particularly helpful, especially if the editor can speak directly to our contributions to the journal. Or if the job involves teaching lots of composition courses, then a recommendation from someone who has observed our teaching and can vouch for our talents will add strength to any teaching claims we might make in other parts of our application.

Of course, those who know us best likely also know our weaknesses, so ask for recommendations only from colleagues or professors who can champion our work unequivocally. "Administrators are used to reading between the lines," writes Natasha Sajé. "When asking someone for a recommendation, you should have a sense that they will write a thoughtful one, and frankly ask them if they will be able to write you a good one."[19] And if we already know that someone has a problem with our work, we shouldn't ask that person for a letter at all.

Curriculum vitae (CV): Anyone pursuing the academic life should maintain a growing CV of professional experience and qualifications. But we should be prepared to adapt that CV to the requirements of a particular job. All CVs start with contact information and education, but depending on the position we are applying for, we may want to shuffle around the order of what appears next. For an associate professor position at a tier-one research institution, we might lead with a list of publications and conference presentations to emphasize our engagement in scholarship. For a community college looking for a multipurpose instructor, we might frontload a list of all the courses we've taught and any teaching awards we've earned.

Teaching philosophy statement: This is a chance to highlight our strengths as teachers—our creative approaches to both instruction and assessment— but also to showcase our awareness of current pedagogical theory and our commitment to individual students. It's not an emotional reflection, not a celebration of the joy of teaching, and not merely a narrative of our best classroom moment. "We don't want the Story of Teaching," writes Karen Kelsky. "We want principles of teaching, and evidence that you exemplify these principles in specific classroom goals and practices."[20]

Kelsky recommends a simple formula: identify a "wide general good" that we hope to accomplish in class. Then describe approaches that we believe help produce this "good," backed up by examples from our own teaching. Then we provide "evidence that the strategies were effective,"[21] and we're done. One page. Simple and direct, with specific examples all along the way. We don't need to present ourselves as perfect teachers, but as committed ones who clearly recognize when a classroom approach is working and how to adapt when it is not.

Diversity and inclusion statement: Colleges and universities seek faculty who are committed to making both the classroom and the larger campus community more inclusive, equitable, and accessible. And as with a teaching statement, there's a significant difference between paying lip-service to vague principles and demonstrating real commitment. A diversity and inclusion statement should emphasize specific experience with diversity and detail concrete steps we've taken to support students from traditionally marginalized groups. We might discuss ways we value diversity in our syllabi or recall a meaningful classroom moment mediating a difficult conversation with students. We should also highlight any specific training we've received or any diversity and inclusion organizations that we support. And if we don't have much experience with diversity, says Tanya Golash-Boza, "then go out and do something. Sign up to be a tutor at an underperforming school, build a house with Habitat for Humanity or incorporate antiracist pedagogy into your teaching."[22] Of course, such efforts will only mean something if they influence how we work in the classroom. Otherwise we're just padding a resume.

The University Hiring Process

Most university hiring cycles include three stages. First, in late fall or early winter, the committee reviews initial applications (typically this means application letters, CVs, letters of recommendation, teaching and diversity statements, and writing samples). Together the committee creates a short list of qualified candidates and then asks those candidates for more application material (this may include sample syllabi, student evaluations, and further writing samples). Based on this second screening the committee may invite a handful of those candidates to participate in preliminary interviews and ultimately invite two or three finalists for a formal campus visit.

Making it through the initial stages of the hiring process requires a stellar application, but everyone knows that a person on paper is not the same thing as a person, well, in person. At joeyfranklin.com/writershustle there are copious links to some of the best online advice about the minutiae of the interview and campus visit process, but our success all comes down to how well we can answer two basic questions: First, are we really as smart as we seem on paper? And second, will our personality and demeanor be a good fit for the department?

If we've landed an interview or a campus visit, it's safe to assume that we are, at least theoretically, the kind of faculty a department is looking for. But in the interview and campus visit process, our job is to remove all doubt. We do this first by doing our research. Get online and get familiar with the university and its mission statement as well as the department and its major initiatives. Learn about creative writing and other course offerings and also extra-curricular activities that align with our interests. It's easier to make an argument that we're the right hire if we already have an idea of how we might be of service in the department.

We should also be ready to talk in specifics about our writing—what we've published and what we're working on. Not only will committees want to hear us use discipline-specific language to talk critically about the craft and theory of creative writing, but they'll want to see how our writing pursuits inform our work in the classroom.

And whether the interview is for a genre-specific position or a more generalist position, we should have in mind specific texts for particular courses and how we might use them in teaching. If I'm a poet, the committee will expect that I can speak at length about the poets and poems that I might teach, but they may also be interested in the texts I'd use to teach fiction, creative nonfiction, or even composition or literature courses. In the hiring process, it can feel like the department is doing the candidate a favor, but if we can help the department see us as a potential asset, it will feel like we are the ones doing them a favor, and the hiring decision becomes simpler.

Another way to show our fit is to demonstrate genuine interest in the faculty, staff, and students we interact with during interviews and visits. If we do our homework ahead of time, we should have lots of questions about the people we meet and the department they work and study in, but we should be equally ready to do some on-the-ground investigation. Find out what faculty and students love about a department and what they don't. Ask faculty about their research and creative projects; ask students about their favorite professors. In the interview and campus visit process, most of the focus is necessarily going to be on the candidate, and that can be exhausting, especially in informal settings—receptions, dinners, and casual conversations. A prepared candidate will be ready to model the collegial give-and-take that every faculty member hopes to find when they show up at work.

Have a Good Plan B

In the middle of all this effort to build a professional portfolio—the writing, publishing, teaching, training, and volunteering—we have to prepare ourselves for the likelihood that it will all be insufficient. There will not be enough jobs for everyone who wants one. There will almost always be candidates who are better qualified than we are. And even when we are qualified and earn an interview and then a campus visit, we may not hit it off with the faculty in a particular department, and the job will go to someone else. And this may happen again and again, over several years while

INTERVIEWING

"THE BEST WAY OUT IS ALWAYS THROUGH" - ROBERT FROST

RESEARCH

SEARCH

- THE POSITION (HOW DOES YOUR EXPERIENCE FIT THE DESCRIPTION?)
- THE PEOPLE (WHO SHARES COMMON PROFESSIONAL INTERESTS?)
- THE ORGANIZATION (HOW DOES YOUR WORK FIT THEIR MISSION?)

RESEARCH NOW = CONFIDENCE LATER

PREPARE

- PRACTICE ANSWERING INTERVIEW QUESTIONS
- PREPARE YOUR OWN QUESTIONS
- WEAR SOMETHING PROFESSIONAL (KEEP THE ATTENTION ON YOU, NOT YOUR CLOTHES)
- ARRIVE EARLY. USE THE BATHROOM, CHECK YOUR ZIPPER, CHECK YOUR HAIR, POP A MINT

GET ADVICE FROM CURRENT EMPLOYEES!

PERFORM

- STAY CALM
- TAKE A BEAT & A BREATH BEFORE ANSWERING
- SPEAK SLOWLY
- SHOW AUTHENTIC INTEREST
- ASK QUESTIONS THAT MATTER (SOMETHING GOOGLE CAN'T TELL YOU)

BE (YOUR BEST) SELF

#1 MOST HIREABLE

FOLLOW-UP

- SEND A THANK-YOU NOTE BE SPECIFIC. WHAT DID YOU LEARN? WHOM WERE YOU GLAD TO MEET?
- REITERATE YOUR GRATITUDE & YOUR INTEREST

REMIND THEM WHY YOU'RE THE RIGHT PERSON FOR THE JOB!

FIGURE 9 *"Interviewing," with an epigraph from Robert Frost,* North of Boston. *New York: Henry Holt and Company, 1915; Bartleby.com, March 2, 2022. 1999. www.bartleby.com/118/.*

we hold down temporary teaching positions and hope for the chips to fall in our favor. Dora Malech once wrote that preparing tenure-track faculty applications was like buying "a very time-consuming lottery ticket."[23] And while the odds aren't quite that bad, faculty hiring is, as Malech says, "part process, and part luck." We put together the best application we can, but in the end, says Malech, "Your materials have to arrive in front of the right people at the right moment," and that's largely beyond our control.

There may come a time when we feel the opportunity cost of chasing a faculty position is too great and we decide to look for something else. And that decision will be easier if we have been preparing for it along the way. Everything we've already said about enhancing and supplementing a liberal arts education holds true for graduate students and for newly minted MFA and PhDs on the job market. We can look to supplementary coursework, internships, research and teaching assistantships, freelance and other employment, and volunteer efforts as well. All those extra-curricular activities will introduce us to a broad variety of professions and professionals. And we can build off that experience and those connections to find meaningful employment.

A FRIEND OF MINE in graduate school used to say, "If this doesn't work out, I can always sell insurance," which is probably true for most of us. But unless we're okay with whatever random industry we can fall into, we better be intentional now about our professional preparation. We better think clearly about our skills and interests and actively seek out opportunities to apply those skills in novel ways. There is a difference, after all, between having an actual plan B while still pursuing our dreams and merely holding in our head the notion of some other plan while we hope our dreams come true.

10.

STAYING IN THE GAME

Let's begin our final chapter with a tale of two writers: we'll call them James and Mari.

James was a promising graduate student at a midwestern university. He seemed to drip with talent, and he impressed his teachers and classmates with everything he turned in. He thrived on the structure of workshops and program requirements, and everyone assumed he'd graduate and go on to make a name for himself as a writer. He finished his thesis—a collection of short stories—and even published one in a well-known magazine. But after graduation he couldn't find a teaching job, and he eventually moved on to a full-time position in marketing. He thinks occasionally about his unpublished collection of stories, and eventually he'll get around to working on them, but when he gets home every night he's tired, and life always seems to get in the way. He's happy enough, and the world will go on spinning even if he never writes another story. But once in a while, usually when he's reading a good book, James gets that itch again, and he's struck by the fact that such an important part of him has lain dormant for so long. *Tomorrow's a good day to start*, he tells himself. *Tomorrow, I'll dust off the laptop and get to work.*

Mari, on the other hand, took a few poetry workshops at a local arts center, and though she never thought seriously about an academic career, she discovered that writing was good for her. It introduced her to great literature, helped her think more clearly, channeled her creative energy, and put her in touch with new friends with writerly sensibilities. After her last workshop, she kept on writing and reading. Her day job keeps her busy, and she doesn't always make time to write, but when she does, it makes a difference. She stays in contact with some of those writerly friends, and they share book recommendations and the occasional finished poem. Recently, Mari found a local writing group that encouraged her to finish a manuscript. She's started attending open-mic nights at a local book store, reading her own work, and meeting other writers in her community. One of them introduced her to a local publisher, and though Mari just received a rejection letter, it felt good to put her work out there, and she's looking forward to getting back to her keyboard.

I should pause here and say that James and Mari are composites, not actual people. But that doesn't mean their situations aren't absolutely common. Most creative writing professors can recall a talented student who dedicated years of school to the writing life only to graduate and leave it all behind. But those professors could also probably name a writer who joined a single writing group or class that changed the trajectory of their lives—not because that writer went on to land some amazing writing job or publish the next great American novel but because that writer embraced a lifelong habit of reading and writing that has helped them live a richer, more satisfying life. Like gardeners, musicians, and woodworkers, writers like this have discovered the value of a craft for its own sake—the challenge of hard work, the promise of regular effort, and the happy consequences of commitment. They come in all shapes and sizes and work in what genre they please. Writing is more than hobby or occupation. It is a way of being in and making sense of the world. The surlier among them might say with Robert Hass, "It's hell writing and it's hell not writing. The only tolerable state is having just written."[1] While those with sunnier dispositions might prefer Anne Lamott: "Writing has so much to give, so much to teach, so many surprises . . . It's like discovering that while you thought you needed the tea ceremony for the caffeine what you really needed was the tea ceremony."[2]

Cultivating such a relationship with writing is hard. Maintaining that relationship over many years is even harder. Workshops end, writing groups fold, communities fizzle out, friendships wither, and life gets in the way. Being a writer means embracing that ebb and flow and learning to adapt. We're talking about resilience of course—grit. And that's what this book has been all about: discovering the habits of mind and work that help a writer foster a meaningful creative life, come what may. And though we've focused much of our attention on getting started as a new writer, these are issues writers face again and again. Thankfully, there are a few principles that can help us adjust, refine, and recommit to those habits and sustain a lifetime of writing in the process.

Routines Are Sacred but Not Etched in Stone

"The day I became a writer was not the day I sold my book, nor the day I was accepted to a la-di-da program," says novelist Ted Thompson. Instead, "it was probably the first time I set an alarm and actually got out of bed, when I went to the kitchen and ground the beans and poured the water, and most importantly when I told myself to sit down and get to work because this mattered."[3]

Thompson became a writer "one day at a time" by creating a routine and making it sacred. But a writing life also requires the flexibility to adjust that routine. An hour a day might work right now, but six months down the road we may only have fifteen minutes. It's our fidelity to keeping a routine, and not its specifics, that ultimately matters. "You find the hours and protect them," says Thompson. "You treat them as important and they become important, you treat your work as valid and it becomes valid."[4]

A Writer's Notebook: Always Helpful, Sometimes a Goldmine

Poet Naomi Shihab Nye likens a writer's notebook to the junk drawer in a kitchen where "we place all the little scraps of things"[5] that we don't know what to do with. And like that kitchen drawer, a well-stocked writing journal will contain all manner of odds and ends that may someday get us out of a writing jam. "If you trust your notebooks, they will give you what you need when you need it," Nye promises. And the keyword here is *trust*. Trust that by jotting down the image, the scene, the character, the question, the odd or pleasing rhythmic line, we're storing it away for some potential future use. Our thoughts gradually accumulate, and when we go back through our notes, mining for inspiration, what we find is not merely the detritus of a junk drawer but a piecemeal record of our mental landscape over time.

As novelist Diana Abu-Jaber describes it, "Reading old journal and outline notes helps me to see what richly layered beings we are."[6] She sees "odd currents . . . repeating words and images, patterns, as if we were each embedded with private themes, symbols that could help unlock the mysteries of our existence." Sporadic note-taking is better than nothing, but a committed journaling practice will help us organize better the chaos of our conscious lives and will provide the raw materials necessary to help turn that chaos into art.

The Tradition Can Inspire Us, but Only If We Know It

When poet Maurice Manning was a student, he came to the "liberating and intimidating" realization that his coursework alone wouldn't introduce him to all the books he needed to know. It was liberating because he knew he was free to read whatever struck his interest. But it was also intimidating because the number of books he hadn't read was so large. And yet, says Manning, by reading his way through the tradition, "I eventually developed a hunger [for the best books] as well as a discipline [for reading them]."[7]

Novelist Janice Fitch has a simple rule for her reading list—only "fiercely good books." And there's no time to waste on "recreational reading," she warns. Instead, "Read work that you really admire; writers who are doing something original, difficult or unique."[8] If we want our reading to have a real positive impact on our writing, Fitch says we must read with urgency. "Study the books you read. Tear them apart. Go to readings, read reviews . . . Talk about what you're reading, what moves you found interesting." To write well is to engage the tradition, to write within it, to expand and explore it, to upend and explode it, but we can't do that unless we first come to know it.

We Will Always Need Other Creative People

For Soraya Duncan, finding room for creativity in her professional life has been largely about listening to herself, figuring out what she really wants to spend her time doing, and surrounding herself with the people that can help her do it.

Duncan started out as a psychology major at Amsterdam University College and only took creative writing courses as a break from her more "serious" coursework. After graduation, she landed a marketing job that was great for her pocketbook, but it came with a lot of drama and not much opportunity for creativity. "I started an Instagram poetry page on the side as catharsis and a self-esteem builder," says Duncan. And through that simple creative outlet she "began to realize that writing, and art in general, was more essential to me than I had previously admitted."[9]

After that realization, she began working more directly with the creatives on her team, throwing around ideas for social media posts, and eventually she approached her boss about making creative work part of her job description. This helped her develop the portfolio she would need a few months later when she applied for and landed a job as a content writer for a major clothing brand.

"You have to have an honest conversation with yourself about money," says Duncan. "If you can be a starving artist, great! If you can't, work toward a day job that will give you what you need to feel safe and accomplished." After that, she says, "take any ethical opportunity someone will give you to write publicly or professionally."

Duncan's work is satisfying, but she's the first to admit that selling clothes places a cap on her creativity. And because she recognized early on that she needed to surround herself with other creative types, she recently enrolled in a screenwriting mentorship where she's working with a local producer on an original TV series. She's not banking on a million-dollar Netflix deal, but the external support has been exactly what she needed to round out her professional life.

All Writing Jobs Are Creative

Few things have the potential to interfere more directly with the writing life than the fact that we all need gainful employment. And as novelist Thomas Mullen reminds us, there is a common belief among some writers "that it's best to have a non-writing day job so that you can magically save your writing energy for nights and weekends."[10] Mullen calls this "perhaps the worst advice" he ever got. Mullen spent his twenties "suffering through right-brain jobs like consulting and nonprofit medical research" where he "toiled unhappily" for years while "hiding my writing life like it was some superhero secret identity." Finally, in his early thirties he took a job as a marketing copywriter.

"Was it as fun as writing novels? No," he writes. "But it was far better than my previous jobs, which treated creativity like some suspect character trait, or sign of insanity." And, he continues, "all jobs take time and energy . . . No matter what you do, you are going to be tired at 6pm. You might as well get tired doing something you're actually good at."

Author and freelance copywriter Amy Berkowitz feels the same way about her "non-creative" work. "Copywriting has actually been very good training for my creative writing,"[11] she tells me. "For one thing, it has cured me of my fear of a blank page." When she's facing a deadline, there's no time for procrastination. "Even if I really don't know where to start, even if I'm feeling overwhelmed or distracted, I have to open up a document and make myself start writing." And even if what comes out is terrible, "I just have to keep going until something clicks. And it always does."

On top of that, her training as a poet has been good for her copywriting. "In both genres, concision is crucial, and the slightest tweak to language can make a big impact." The difference, of course, is ego. "At the end of the day, my name isn't on [marketing copy]." This means even if she's writing at work, she can reserve the emotional investment for personal projects, which, she says, "contain my heart and soul."

Not All Writing Jobs Are Creative Enough

Chris Maier is a short story writer turned brand storyteller who has, over the past twenty years, helped revamp a university alumni magazine, earned an MFA in fiction, written college guidebooks for Princeton Review, worked as a creative director at a mid-size branding agency, and twice hung out his own shingle as a marketing consultant. And while his professional life serves as a model for making creative skills work in a professional world, what Maier can really teach us is the value of channeling our creative energy and not letting our day job limit our creative possibilities.

When Maier started his own company, he had typical business goals about offering a valuable service for his clients, but he also wanted "space to invest time into non-client related creative projects." In 2015, he established a boutique performing arts organization that showcased local Washington DC, talent at intimate venues around the city. He called it "Little Salon," and it shut down during the 2020 pandemic, but not before hosting more than fifty events all over the DC metro area. "We'll cram 100 people shoulder-to-shoulder into a living room and send people home at night with not only exposure to new arts and artists," says Maier, "but also (hopefully) a few new acquaintances they may never have bumped into otherwise." Even though Maier's job isn't a completely "creative" endeavor, he's recognized how much he values the arts and so has made a space within his work life to make the arts possible.

In addition, he's made time to keep writing, and he's recently spent three years shooting and editing a documentary film about "an outlaw racetrack in rural Virginia." Maier loves the creative aspects of his day job, but he says, "if the professional work doesn't always scratch that creative itch, it's crucial to find time and space to make that creative work happen."[12]

"HOW WE SPEND OUR days is, of course, how we spend our lives," writes Annie Dillard. "What we do with this hour, and that one, is what we are doing."[13] Resilient writers know that the writing life comes slowly, with patience, persistence, and enough charity to forgive ourselves when we fail. But they also know that such a life must be intentionally developed.

None of these writers stumbled into their creative lives. Nor did any of the dozens of other writers we've heard from over the course of this book. Instead, through a process of trial and error, they have discovered the approaches that keep them working. They have established rich habits of reading and note-taking that become sources of inspiration. They have figured out what kind of community they need and where to find it. They have cultivated professional identities that support and enhance their creative inclinations. And they have learned the importance of remaining flexible in the face of change. This is the writer's hustle—not careerism or networking. Not schmoozing or selling out. But knowing what's good for us as writers and having the discipline necessary to make it happen.

Many of us know a writer who has lived this way—an enviable model of disciplined creative living who has maintained their craft over decades. We hold them up as polestars, proof that there's value in so much solitary scribbling. One such writer for me has been my father-in-law, Michael Fitzgerald, who passed away a few months before I could finish this book. Despite his lifetime of writing, most folks have never heard of him.

THE WRITER'S HUSTLE

A SELF-EVALUATION

"NOTORIETY AND MEDIOCRITY ARE OFTEN INTERCHANGEABLE TERMS."
– EDITH WHARTON

- [ ] I READ WIDELY TO KEEP MYSELF INFORMED AND INSPIRED.
- [ ] I USE A RELIABLE NOTETAKING SYSTEM TO RECORD MY DAILY THOUGHTS & OBSERVATIONS.
- [ ] I SET REALISTIC, MEASURABLE GOALS FOR MY WRITING.
- [ ] I HAVE A ROUTINE THAT HELPS ME MEET MY WRITING GOALS.
- [ ] I USE THE INTERNET TO BUILD A WRITING COMMUNITY AND EXPAND MY READING.
- [ ] I SEEK OUT CRITICISM FROM PEERS, AND TRUST CRITIQUE AS PART OF THE WRITING PROCESS.
- [ ] I LOOK FOR MENTORS WHO CAN MODEL NOT ONLY WAYS OF WORKING, BUT ALSO WAYS OF LIVING.
- [ ] I SUPPORT OTHER WRITERS BY PARTICIPATING IN MY LOCAL WRITING COMMUNITY.
- [ ] I TRUST THE PROCESS—THAT GREAT WRITING HAPPENS SLOWLY, ONE DAY AT A TIME.
- [ ] I SUBMIT WORK WHEN IT'S READY, AND I USE REJECTION AS PART OF THE WRITING PROCESS.
- [ ] IF I'M IN A CREATIVE WRITING PROGRAM, I'VE ALSO GOT A BACK-UP PLAN.
- [ ] I REVIEW MY GOALS & ADJUST MY HABITS AND ROUTINES TO CONTINUE MAKING PROGRESS.
- [ ] I FORGIVE MYSELF FOR FALLING SHORT TODAY, AND THEN GET BACK AT IT TOMORROW.

FIGURE 10 *"The Writer's Hustle: A Self-Evaluation," with an epigraph from Edith Wharton,* The Writing of Fiction, *(New York: Scribners, 1925), p. 19, March 2, 2022, https://archive.org/details/writingoffiction0000whar.*

He got his start as an English major in the early 1980s and went on to a technical writing gig after graduation. He spent the next several decades producing technical material, user manuals, and other corporate copy. He also published freelance articles, wrote several computer programming manuals that are still in print, self-published a kid's book, and, in his fifties, used Amazon Kindle Direct Publishing to put out several of his long-term personal projects, including some books on religion, positive living, and a young adult novel that he'd been working on for years.

What always impressed me though was the work that Mike did beneath the surface of his professional writing life. He volunteered to teach creative writing at an elementary school. He periodically reenrolled in college literature and writing courses to stay up on trends, and he worked as a writing coach—sometimes for pay, sometimes simply because he believed in a project. He handwrote and illustrated personalized board books for his grandchildren, wrote poetry for dying friends, and sent me occasional late night texts to share neologisms that made him laugh (my favorite was "metroglyph," which was his novel word for graffiti). Most impressive though, for his entire adult life, Mike kept a journal—more than forty volumes from the early 1970s up until the day before he died, handwritten and numbered; twenty-thousand-plus pages of daily observations, questions, worries, and writing ideas.

Mike always told me that it was his journals that taught him how to write, and it was his journals in the end that kept him going. Mike contracted Covid-19 in the early months of 2020 and never really recovered. Over the next year and a half, long-haul Covid exacerbated an autoimmune disorder which in turn led to chronic fatigue and short-term disability because he could no longer make it through a full day's work. But he was still writing. He was helping a friend with a book, making marketing notes for his own work, and right up until the week before he passed away he was still filling his journal with notes about a sequel to his YA novel. Writing didn't always make him the money he hoped it would (and he even drove a dump truck for a few years during the great recession), but writing is what he loved and what he always came back to. He took one day at a time and trusted that writing would provide what it always had—clarity, peace, a sense of adventure, and a glimpse into himself that few other things could offer.

Shortly after recovering from his initial bout with Covid-19, Mike wrote in his journal. "Run every day. If you can't run, walk fast. If you can't walk fast, walk as fast as you can. If you can't walk, limp. If you can't limp, crawl. If you can't crawl, roll. If you can't roll, imagine you are running." And I don't think there's a better sentiment we could end on. We may not always measure up to someone else's idea of what it means to be a writer, but by recommitting on a daily basis to our own goals and pursuing them with this kind of determination, keeping ourselves humble and teachable along the way, then no matter what challenges we face, inspiration will come and the satisfaction of a creative life along with it.

NOTES

Introduction

1 Ernest Hemingway, quoted in "The Art of Fiction XXI: Ernest Hemingway," by George Plimpton, *Paris Review*, no. 18 (Spring 1958): 67.

2 Joan Didion, *Slouching Toward Bethlehem* (New York: Farrar, Straus, and Giroux, 2008), 139.

3 Jeff Baker, "The Hottest Writing Group in Portland," *The Oregonian*, June 27, 2010.

4 Thomas Wentworth Higginson, "Emily Dickinson's Letters," *The Atlantic Monthly*, October 1891, https://www.theatlantic.com/magazine/archive/1891/10/emily-dickinsons-letters/306524.

5 Matthew Weaver and Mark Brown, "Man Book Winner's Debut Novel Rejected Nearly 80 Times," *The Guardian*, October 14, 2015, https://www.theguardian.com/books/2015/oct/14/man-booker-prize-marlon-james-debut-novel-rejected-nearly-80-times.

6 Emily Temple, "'Fear Is Good Quality Control,' Colson Whitehead on the Writer's Life," Lithub, March 27, 2018, https://lithub.com/fear-is-good-quality-control-colson-whitehead-on-the-writers-life.

Chapter 1

1 Henry James, *The Art of Fiction and Other Essays* (New York: Oxford University Press, 1948), 11.

2 Ursula K. Le Guin, "When to Bend, When to Break," *Los Angeles Times*, January 5, 2003, https://www.latimes.com/archives/la-xpm-2003-jan-05-bk -leguin5-story.html.

3 Lee Child, "UKA Interview with Lee Child," UKAuthors.com, January 8, 2022, https://ukauthors.com/uka-articles-parent/wabd-interview-with-lee-child.

4 Margaret Atwood, *Dancing Girls and Other Stories* (Toronto: Seal Books, 1977), 200.

5 Jewell Parker Rhodes, *The African American Guide to Writing and Publishing Nonfiction* (New York: Broadway Books, 2001), 37.

6 Tim Denevi, personal interview, January 29, 2020.

7 Jodi Picoult, "This Writer's Life: Jodi Picoult: The Fact Behind Fiction," *Writer's Digest*, March 11, 2008, https://www.writersdigest.com/writing -articles/this-writers-life-jodi-picoultthe-fact-behind-fiction.

8 Martine Leavitt, personal interview, January 30, 2020.

9 Anne Lamott, *Bird By Bird: Some Instructions on Writing and Life* (New York: Anchor Books, 1994), 63.

10 Natalie Goldberg, *Writing Down the Bones: Freeing the Writer Within* (Boston: Shambhala, 1986), 44.

11 Heather Hammond, private email correspondence, 2020, used with permission.

12 Ibid.

13 Hugh. D. Young and Roger Freedman, *University Physics with Modern Physics 14th Edition* (New York: Pearson, 2015), 212.

14 Ibid., 500.

15 Robert Resnick, David Halliday and Jearl Walker, *Fundamentals of Physics* (Hoboken: Wiley, 2013). 89.

16 Roger Freedman, personal interview, December 29, 2020.

17 Hugh John Vaughen Campbell, *Room Notes by The 6th Earl of Cawdor* (Nairn: Cawdor Castle Ltd., 2005), 8.

18 Ibid., 17.

19 Ibid., 20.

20 Ibid., 23.

21 Ibid., 22.

22 Jaron Lanier, *Ten Arguments for Deleting Your Social Media Accounts Right Now* (New York: Henry Holt, 2018), 7.

23 Francesco Cirillo, *The Pomodoro Technique: The Acclaimed Time-Management System That Has Transformed How We Work* (New York: Crown, 2018).

24 Joyce Carol Oates, celestialtimepiece.com.

25 Annie Dillard, "Write Till You Drop," *New York Times*, May 28, 1989, https://www.nytimes.com/1989/05/28/books/write-till-you-drop.html.

26 Ibid.

27 Jeff Sharlet, *Brilliant Darkness: A Book of Strangers* (New York: Norton, 2020), 7.

28 Steven Spatz, "Do Authors Really Need To Blog?" *The Writing Cooperative*, July 5, 2018, https://writingcooperative.com/do-authors-really-need-to-blog-94e78a8f7cde.

29 B. Zelkovich, "Fanfiction–Pros and Cons," *To Write These Words Down . . .*, February 10, 2018, https://iemergedinlondonrain.wordpress.com/2018/02/10/fanfiction-pros-and-cons/.

30 Julie Beck, "What Fan Fiction Teaches That the Classroom Doesn't," *The Atlantic*, October 1, 2019, https://www.theatlantic.com/education/archive/2019/10/how-fanfiction-improves-writing/599197.

31 Katie Davis and Cecilia Aragon, quoted by Stephanie Burt, "The Promise and Potential of Fan Fiction," *The New Yorker*, August 23, 2017, https://www.newyorker.com/books/page-turner/the-promise-and-potential-of-fan-fiction.

32 Zelkovich, "Fanfiction – Pros and Cons."

33 Burt, "The Promise and Potential of Fan Fiction."

34 Lanier, *Ten Arguments*, 143.

35 Jonathan Franzen, "Jonathan Franzen: The Internet Should Be Really Strictly Regulated," interview by Prachi Gupta, *Salon,* October 24, 2013, https://www.salon.com/2013/10/24/jonathan_franzen_the_internet_should_be_really_strictly_regulated.

36 William Zinnserr, *Writing to Learn: How to Write—and Think—Clearly About Any Subject at All* (New York: Harper & Row, 1988), 49.

Chapter 2

1 Ira Sukrungruang, personal interview, July 1, 2020.

2 See D. G. Myers, "The Rise of Creative Writing," *Journal of the History of Ideas* 54, no. 2 (1993): 294.

3 Junot Diaz, "MFA vs. POC," *The New Yorker,* April 30, 2014, https://www.newyorker.com/books/page-turner/mfa-vs-poc.

4 Jen Corrigan, "How Men Police Women's Anger in Writing Workshops," *Bitch,* October 22, 2018, https://www.bitchmedia.org/article/men-police-womens-anger-writing-workshops.

5 Ana Valens, "Why We Must Bring LGBT Writing into the Creative Writing Classroom," *Pride,* September 14, 2016, https://pride.com/backtoschool/2016/9/14/why-we-must-bring-lgbt-writing-creative-writing-classroom.

6 Alyssa Radtke, "When Being a Disabled Writer Means Being an Educator," *Lit Hub*, January 29, 2018, https://lithub.com/when-being-a-disabled-writer-means -being-an-educator.

7 Rosalie Morales Kearns, "Voice of Authority: Theorizing Creative Writing Pedagogy," *College Composition and Communication* 60, no. 4 (2009): 794.

8 Donald Hall, "Poetry and Ambition," *Kenyon Review* 5, no. 4 (1983): 98.

9 Sarah Jefferis, personal interview, February 7, 2020.

10 Robert Pinsky, quoted in "Robert Pinsky Speaks at the Ethel L. Handley Annual Reading," by Silvia Culter, Brigham Young University College of Humanities, October 3, 2014, https://humanities.byu.edu/robert-pinsky-at-the -ethel-l-handley-annual-reading.

11 Wendy Bishop, *Released into Language: Options for Teaching Creative Writing* (Urbana: National Council of Teachers of English, 1991), 49.

12 Ann Patchett, *This Is the Story of a Happy Marriage* (New York: HarperCollins, 2013), 29.

13 Jim Nelson, "A Fourth Alternative to the Iowa Writing Workshop Format," *j -nelson.net*, June 2, 2015, https://j-nelson.net/2015/06/a-fourth-alternative-to -the-iowa-writing-workshop-format.

14 Rachel Toor, "The Writers' Workshop at Work," *The Chronicle of Higher Education,* April 5, 2011, https://www.chronicle.com/article/the-writers -workshop-at-work.

15 Rachel Toor, "A Writing Group of Two," *The Chronicle of Higher Education*, December 16, 2010, https://www.chronicle.com/article/a-writing-group-of -two.

16 Claire P. Curtis, "The Rules of Writing Group," *The Chronicle of Higher Education*, March 24, 2011, https://www.chronicle.com/article/the-rules-of -writing-group.

17 Ibid.

18 Xu Xi, personal interview, November 11, 2020.

19 Liz Lerman, quoted in "Introduction to CRP." Guildhall School of Drama. YouTube video, 5:55, May 31, 2016, https://www.youtube.com/watch?v =4I7IH6oYWbw.

20 Kearns, "Voice of Authority," 793.

21 Noor Naga and Robert McGill, "Negotiating Cultural Difference in Creative Writing Workshops: Close Reading Translations and Interpretive Diversity," *Pedagogy* 18, no. 1 (2018): 75.

22 Lerman, quoted in "Responders Questions." Guildhall School of Drama. YouTube video, 8:21, May 26, 2016, https://www.youtube.com/watch?v=Ge -gghwoTsw&t=10s.

23 Madison Smartt Bell, quoted in "Method and Madness in the Creative Writing Workshop," by Michael Loyd Gray, *The English Journal* 89, no. 1 (1999): 17.

24 Noor and McGill, "Cultural Difference in Creative Writing," 82.

25 Svetlana Mintcheva, "Structures of Power and the Ethical Limits of Speech,"
    truthdig.com, May 25, 2017, https://www.truthdig.com/articles/structures-of
    -power-and-the-ethical-limits-of-speech.

26 Jarune Uwujaren, "The Difference Between Cultural Exchange and
    Cultural Appropriation," *Everyday Feminism*, September 30, 2013, https://
    everydayfeminism.com/2013/09/cultural-exchange-and-cultural-appropriation.

27 Rivka Galchen and Anna Holmes, "What Distinguishes Cultural Exchange
    from Cultural Appropriation?", *The New Yorker*, June 8, 2017, https://www
    .nytimes.com/2017/06/08/books/review/bookends-cultural-appropriation.html.

28 Ibid.

29 Nisi Shawl, "Appropriate Cultural Appropriation," *writingtheother.com*, August
    20, 2016, https://writingtheother.com/appropriate-cultural-appropriation.

30 Ixty Quintanilla, "Cultural Appropriation in Fiction: Here Are Some Tips
    to Consider When Your Writing Includes Different Cultures," *Everyday
    Feminism,* April 9, 2018, https://everydayfeminism.com/2018/04/cultural
    -appropriation-fiction.

31 Jeannette Ng, "Cultural Appropriation for the Worried Writer: Some
    Practical Advice," Medium.com, October 29, 2018, https://medium.com/@
    nettlefish/cultural-appropriation-for-the-worried-writer-some-practical-advice
    -ac21710685e3.

32 Kit De Waal, "Don't Dip Your Pen in Someone Else's Blood: Writers and 'The
    Other,'" *The Irish Times,* June 30, 2018, https://www.irishtimes.com/culture/books
    /don-t-dip-your-pen-in-someone-else-s-blood-writers-and-the-other-1.3553819.

33 Julie Berry, quoted in "Confessions of a Sensitivity Reader," by Marjorie Ingall,
    Tablet, March 7, 2019, https://www.tabletmag.com/sections/community/
    articles/confessions-of-a-sensitivity-reader.

34 Balogun Ojetade, "RESEARCH, RESEARCH, RESEARCH! Avoiding Cultural
    Appropriation in Steampunk," *Chronicles of Harriet*, February 6, 2015, https://
    chroniclesofharriet.com/2015/02/06/appropriation.

35 Svetlana Mintcheva, "Writer's Imagination vs. Cultural Appropriation: In
    Search of Common Ground," *Salon*. September 26, 2016. https://www.salon
    .com/2016/09/26/writers-imagination-vs-cultural-appropriation-in-search-of
    -common-ground/.

36 Melissa Febos, personal interview, April 14, 2020.

Chapter 3

1 Stephen King, *On Writing: A Memoir of the Craft* (New York: Scribner, 2000),
   147.

2 Roxane Gay, "Eight Questions Writers Should Ask Themselves," Association of
   Writers and Writing Programs, November 2013, https://www.awpwriter.org/
   magazine_media/writers_notebook_view/5/the_eight_questions_writers_should
   _ask_themselves.

3   John Poch, personal interview, March 22, 2021.

4   Sara Jefferis, personal interview, February 7, 2020.

5   Melissa Febos, personal interview, April 14, 2020.

6   Tim Denevi, personal interview, January 29, 2020.

7   Juli Vick, personal interview, April 2, 2021.

8   Dinty W. Moore, personal interview, March 30, 2021.

9   Morgan Harding, "Notes from a Bookseller: A Seat at the Table," Politcs-prose
    .com, January 11, 2022, https://www.politics-prose.com/notes-bookseller-seat
    -table.

10 Jaron Lanier, *Ten Arguments for Deleting Your Social Media Accounts Right
    Now* (New York: Henry Holt, 2018), 18.

11 Carmen Maria Machado, quoted in "Don't @ Me," by Heather Schwedel,
    Slate, January 31, 2019, https://slate.com/culture/2019/01/authors-criticism
    -books-twitter-mentions-tagging.html.

12 Laura Miller, "In Praise of Reader Reviews," *Slate*, September 8, 2016, https://
    slate.com/culture/2016/09/a-professional-book-critic-in-praise-of-amazon
    -reader-reviews.html.

13 Lewis Hyde, *The Gift: How the Creative Spirit Transforms the World*
    (Edinburgh: Canongate, 2007), xiv.

14 Janet Hulstrand, "How to Write a Fair (and Helpful) Book Review on Amazon
    (or Anywhere)," Janethulstrand.com, October 6, 2020, https://janethulstrand
    .com/2020/10/06/how-to-write-a-fair-and-helpful-book-review-on-amazon-or
    -anywhere.

15 Neal Wooten, "Tips for Writing Amazon Reviews," *Huff Post*, May 27, 2015,
    https://www.huffpost.com/entry/tips-for-writing-amazon-r_b_6959118.

16 Febos, personal interview.

Chapter 4

1   Mark Ford, "Ezra Pound and the Drafts of *The Waste Land*," British Library,
    December 13, 2016, https://www.bl.uk/20th-century-literature/articles/ezra
    -pound-and-the-drafts-of-the-waste-land.

2   Christopher Ricks and Jim McCue, "What Happened to the Original Version
    of *The Waste Land*? One of Literature's 'Minor Mysteries,'" *Lit Hub*,
    December 19, 2018, https://lithub.com/what-happened-to-the-original-version
    -of-the-waste-land.

3   Ibid.

4   Janet Fitch, personal interview, February 14, 2020.

5   José Orduña, personal interview, January 24, 2020.

6   Alexander Chee, "Annie Dillard and the Writing Life," *The Morning News*,
    October 16, 2009, https://themorningnews.org/article/annie-dillard-and-the
    -writing-life.

7 Rick Moody, "Writers and Mentors," *The Atlantic,* August 2005, https://www.theatlantic.com/magazine/archive/2005/08/writers-and-mentors/304101.

8 Rick Moody, quoted in "Writers and Mentors and What Happens in Between' by Miranda Hill," *Hazlitt,* March 12, 2013. https://hazlitt.net/feature/writers-and-mentors-and-what-happens-between.

9 Moody, "Writers and Mentors."

10 Tracy K. Smith, quoted in *Women Poets on Mentorship*, edited by Arielle Greenburg and Rachel Zucker (Iowa City: University of Iowa Press, 2008), 235.

11 Alissa Nutting, quoted in *A Manner of Being: Writers on Their Mentors*, edited by Annie Liontas and Jeff Parker (Amherst: University of Massachusetts Press, 2015), 218.

12 Ibid., 217.

13 Kathy Lou Schultz, quoted in *Women Poets on Mentorship*, 208.

14 Ibid., 210.

15 "1855–1865: The Writing Years," *EmilyDickinsonMuseum.org*, January 7, 2022, https://www.emilydickinsonmuseum.org/emily-dickinson/biography/emily-dickinson-the-writing-years-1855-1865.

16 Thomas Wentworth Higginson, "Emily Dickinson's Letters," *The Atlantic Monthly*, October 1891, https://www.theatlantic.com/magazine/archive/1891/10/emily-dickinsons-letters/306524.

17 E. J. Levy, quoted in "How to Be a Good Literary Citizen: The Best Form of Networking,'" by Joey Franklin, *Poets & Writers*, November/December 2013, 100.

18 Spencer Hyde, personal interview, February 17, 2021.

19 Neil Aitken, "POC Mentorship & Community: On Seeking and Not Finding," *De-Canon*, May 13, 2017, https://www.de-canon.com/blog/2017/5/13/poc-mentorship-on-seeking-the-hermit-and-not-finding-them-in.

20 Ibid.

21 "What is Kundiman," Kundiman.org, January 7, 2022, http://www.kundiman.org/what-is-kundiman.

22 Aitken, "POC Mentorship & Community."

23 Ibid.

24 Daphne Gottlieb, quoted. In *Women Poets on Mentorship*, 47.

25 Aimee Nezhukumatathil quoted in *Women Poets on Mentorship*, 142.

26 Paisley Rekdal, "On Writing Mentors," *Anapessimistic*, October 15, 2011, http://paisleyrekdal.blogspot.com/2011/10/on-writing-mentors.html.

27 Ibid.

28 Tony Hoagland, quoted in *A Manner of Being*, 201.

29 Ibid., 202.

30 Ibid., 203.

Chapter 5

1 Jason Brick, "What Is a Writer's Workshop? An Insider's Guide to Attending Writing Events," TCK Publishing, January 14, 2022, https://www.tckpublishing.com/how-to-get-the-most-from-writers-conferences.

2 Don George quoted in "How to Make the Most of Any Writing Conference," by Linda Formichelli, *Writer's Digest*, October 22, 2014, https://www.writersdigest.com/publishing-faqs/how-to-make-the-most-of-any-writing-conference.

3 Courtney Maum, "So, You're Going to a Writers' Conference?," *Tin House*, April 5, 2012. https://tinhouse.com/so-youre-going-to-a-writers-conference.

4 Sandra Beasley, quoted in "What's the Deal with Writing Residencies? The Blunt Instrument on the Ins and Outs of Residencies for Authors," by Elisa Gabbert, *Electric Literature*, March 27, 2017. https://electricliterature.com/whats-the-deal-with-writing-residencies.

5 See the Western Literature Association, westernlit.org.

6 See the Association of Writers and Writing Programs, www.awpwriter.org.

7 See NonfictioNow, www.nonfictionow.org.

8 See "How Events are Selected," *AWP*, January 28, 2022, https://www.awpwriter.org/awp_conference/event_proposals_selection.

9 Julie Zigoris, "How to Make the Most of a Writing Conference: Eight Tips to Prepare You for a Successful Writing Conference," *Writing Cooperative*, September 29, 2019, https://writingcooperative.com/how-to-make-the-most-of-a-writing-conference-e984107e3006.

10 Bob Hostetler, "Seven Tips for Your Next Writers' Conference," *Steve Laube Agency*, January 24, 2018, https://stevelaube.com/seven-tips-next-writers-conference.

11 Cathy C. Hall, "Top Tips for Writer's Conference Attendees," *The Muffin*, March 14, 2018, https://muffin.wow-womenonwriting.com/2018/03/top-tips-for-writers-conference.html.

12 John Peragine, "Tips for Effective Networking at a Writer's Conference," *Writer's Digest*, July 2, 2019, https://www.writersdigest.com/writing-conferences/10-tips-for-effective-networking-at-a-writers-conference.

13 Brian Klems, "Nine Ways to Get the Most Out of Your Writing Residency," *Writer's Digest*, September 24, 2015, https://www.writersdigest.com/publishing-faqs/9-ways-to-get-the-most-out-of-your-writing-residency.

14 Rich Smith, "AWP: How to Attend without Really Attending," *City Arts Magazine*, February 14, 2014, https://www.cityartsmagazine.com/awp-how-attend-without-really-attending.

15 Kerrie Flanagan, "How to Pitch to an Agent at a Writer's Conference," *Wow!*, January 14, 2022, https://wow-womenonwriting.com/35-How2-PitchAgent.html.

16 Zigoris, "How to Make the Most of a Writing Conference."

17 Cathay Mazak, "Episode Twenty: The Benefits of Writing Retreats and How to Find One that Works for You," CathayMazak.com, February 4, 2020, https://

www.cathymazak.com/episode20-the-benefits-of-writing-retreats-and-how-to
-find-one-that-works-for-you.

18 Marisa Mohi, "Five Things I Learned from My First Writer's Retreat,"
MarisaHohi.com, January 14, 2022, https://marisamohi.com/my-first-writers
-retreat.

Chapter 6

1 Penguin India 2007.

2 Anjum Hasan, personal interview, May 16, 2021.

3 Tom Provost, personal interview, April 22, 2020.

4 Chris Baty, *No Plot? No Problem!* (San Francisco: Chronicle Books, 2004), 27.

5 Haruki Murakami, "Haruki Murakami: The Art of Fiction no. 182," interview
by John Way, *The Paris Review,* no. 170 (Summer 2004): 130.

6 Kimberly Johnson, personal interview, May 17, 2021.

7 Kirstin Chen, personal interview, November 18, 2021.

8 Michael Lavers, personal interview, January 1, 2022.

9 ire'ne lara silva, personal interview, May 25, 2021.

10 Tonya Abari, personal interview, May 26, 2021.

11 Ann Dee Ellis, personal interview, May 18, 2021.

12 BJ Fogg, "Better Control of Your Emotions Will Help You Create Better
Habits," *Time*, December 30, 2019, https://time.com/5756833/better-control
-emotions-better-habits.

13 Ibid.

14 Bec Evans, "How to Use Rewards to Keep Writing," *Prolifiko,* June 22, 2021,
https://prolifiko.com/use-rewards-to-keep-writing.

15 Ian Rankin, quoted in "On Writing: Authors Reveal the Secrets of Their
Craft," *The Guardian,* March 25, 2011, https://www.theguardian.com/
books/2011/mar/26/authors-secrets-writing.

16 Erika L. Sanchez, "An Interview with Erika Sanchez," by Harriet Staff, *Poetry
Foundation,* December 18, 2012, https://www.poetryfoundation.org/harriet
-books/2012/12/an-interview-with-erika-l-sanchez.

17 Stephen King, *On Writing: A Memoir of the Craft* (New York: Scribner,
2000), 37.

18 George Saunders, "George Saunders: The WD Interview," by Tyler Moss,
Writer's Digest, May 9, 2018, https://www.writersdigest.com/be-inspired/wd
-interview-george-saunders-structure-outlining-lincoln-in-the-bardo.

19 Marilynne Robinson, "Marilynne Robinson on Finding the Right Word," *New
York Times*, September 22, 2017, https://www.nytimes.com/2017/09/22/books/
review/marilynne-robinson-on-finding-the-right-word.html.

20 Jericho Brown, "Interview with Jericho Brown," by Marian Kaufman, *Bayou
Magazine*, January 1, 2022, https://bayoumagazine.org/interview-with-jericho
-brown.

21 Lauren Kay Johnson, personal interview, March 19, 2021.

22 Kitty Fields, "Why Writer's Block Doesn't Exist and How You Can Beat It," *Owlcation*, December 9, 2018, https://owlcation.com/humanities/Why-Writers-Block-Doesnt-Exist.

23 Kathleen Sumpton, "Attention Writers: The Myth of Writer's Block," *The Artifice*, July 18, 2015, https://the-artifice.com/myth-of-writers-block.

24 Ashley Shannon, "Writer's Block Doesn't Exist," *Ashley, On Writing*, September 20, 2020, https://medium.com/ashley-on-writing/writers-block-doesn-t-exist-f742fcde7d75.

25 Robert McKee, quoted in *StoryCraft: The Complete Guide to Writing Narrative Nonfiction*, by Jack Hart (Chicago: University of Chicago Press, 2011), 144.

26 Jericho Brown, "Interview with Jericho Brown."

27 A. J. Jacobs, "A. J. Jacobs: How I Write," interview by Noah Charney, *The Daily Beast,* July 11, 2017, https://www.thedailybeast.com/aj-jacobs-how-i-write.

28 Brandon Sanderson, "Can You Go into Depth about Outlining?" brandonsanderson.com, January 2, 2022, https://faq.brandonsanderson.com/knowledge-base/can-you-go-into-depth-about-outlining.

29 Daisy Johnson, "Web Exclusive Interview: Daisy Johnson," by Erin McReynolds, *American Short Fiction*, April 24, 2017, https://americanshortfiction.org/web-exclusive-interview-daisy-johnson.

30 Maggie Smith, "Maggie Smith: On Motherhood, Her Writing Process and Why She Needs Poetry," interview by Kailey Brennan, *Write or Die Tribe*, December 22, 2018, https://www.writeordietribe.com/author-interviews/interview-with-maggie-smith.

31 Leslie Jamison, "A Conversation with Leslie Jamison," interview by Rachel Toliver, *Image Journal*, January 3, 2022, https://imagejournal.org/article/leslie-jamison.

32 ire'ne lara silva, personal interview.

33 Leslie Wibberely, "Beta Readers: What You Need to Know," medium.com, May 25, 2019, https://lawibberley.medium.com/beta-readers-29db8a54db59.

34 Anne Pancake, "Reading How You're Read: The Art of Evaluating Criticism," *Poets & Writers*, May 1, 2007, https://www.pw.org/content/reading_how_you039re_read_art_evaluating_criticism.

35 Sheila Heti, "Sheila Heti on the Importance of Finding Trusted Readers," *Lit Hub*, November 6, 2020, https://lithub.com/sheila-heti-on-the-importance-of-finding-trusted-readers.

36 Lisa Olstein, personal interview, May 24, 2020.

37 Salman Rushdie, "Life's Work: An Interview with Salman Rushdie," by Alison Beard, *Harvard Business Review*, September 2015, https://hbr.org/2015/09/lifes-work-salman-rushdie.

38 Tanaz Bhathena, quoted in "Four Ways to Take Criticism Like a Pro," by Robert Lee Brewer, *Writer's Digest*, 2016.

39 Pancake, "Reading How You're Read."

40 Leigh Shulman, "Your Writing Needs Feedback: This is How to Give and Get it," leighshulman.com, February 15, 2019, https://leighshulman.com/give-and -get-feedback.

41 Susan Breen, "Nine Strategies for Handling Criticism as a Writer," *Writer Magazine*, October 10, 2019, https://www.writermag.com/writing-inspiration/ the-writing-life/handling-criticism.

42 Scott Francis, "Mistake 45: Listening to Too Much Feedback," *Writer's Digest*, September 9, 2009, https://www.writersdigest.com/improve-my-writing/ mistake-45-listening-to-too-much-feedback.

43 Tabitha Blankenbiller, "My Thesis is Not a Book: Confessions of a Lutheran Schoolgirl," *Brevity*, April 26, 2012, https://brevitymag.com/craft-essays/my -thesis-is-not-a-book-confessions-of-a-lutheran-schoolgirl.

44 Micah Cozzens, personal interview, January 3, 2021.

45 Tony Earley, personal Interview, November 18, 2021.

46 Jennifer Emerson, "Strategy and the Reading List," in *Now What? The Creative Writer's Guide to Success After the MFA*, edited by Michael Bayer (Connecticut: Fairfield University Press, 2014), 49.

Chapter 7

1 Joe Oestreich, quoted in "Submit that Manuscript! Why Sending Out Your Work is so Important," by Joey Franklin, *Poets & Writers Magazine*, July/ August 2017, 66. Several portions of this chapter appeared first in slightly different form in this article.

2 Ibid., 67.

3 Ibid.

4 Ibid.

5 Ibid., 68.

6 Ibid.

7 Robert Lee Brewer, "How to Write Successful Queries for Any Genre of Writing," *Writer's Digest*, September 16, 2019, https://www.writersdigest .com/publishing-insights/how-to-write-successful-queries-for-any-genre-of -writing.

8 clmp.org.

9 Anis Shivani, "Poetry Book Contests Should Be Abolished," *Huff Post*, August 2, 2011, https://www.huffpost.com/entry/poetry-book-contests_b_858819.

10 Bailey Cunningham, quoted in "A Look Inside the System of Competition," by Joey Franklin, *Poets & Writers Magazine*, May/June 2019, 56.

11 Christina Ham, "Do I Really Need an Agent?" Playwright's Center, January 4, 2022, https://pwcenter.org/playwriting-toolkit/do-i-need-agent.

12 Mary Sue Price, "Communicating with Theaters: Letters of Inquiry, Cover Letters, Follow-Up Emails," Playwright's Center, January 5, 2022, https://

pwcenter.org/playwriting-toolkit/communicating-theaters-letters-inquiry-cover
-letters-follow-emails.

13 See wgaeast.org.

14 Thomas Lennon and Robert Ben Garrant, *Writing Movies for Fun and Profit:
How We Made a Billion Dollars at the Box Office and You Can, Too!* (New
York: Simon and Schuster, 2011), 11.

15 Chris DeBlasio, "Sending Out Your Script: How to Get Your Movie Script into
the Right Hands," chrisdeblasio.com, April 25, 2019, https://chrisdeblasio.com
/2019/04/25/sending-script-get-movie-script-right-hands.

16 Jeanne Veillette Bowerman, "Take Two: Ways to Submit Your Story to
Hollywood," *Writer's Digest,* June 5, 2019, https://www.writersdigest.com/
write-better-fiction/take-two-ways-to-submit-your-story-to-hollywood.

17 Ken Miyamoto, "Writing the Perfect Query Letter for Your Scripts," *Screen
Craft,* August 13, 2018, https://screencraft.org/blog/writing-the-perfect-query
-letter-for-your-scripts.

18 Noam Kroll, "How to Write the Perfect Logline: And Why It's As Important
as Your Screenplay," *Indie Wire,* January 6, 2014, https://www.indiewire.com
/feature/how-to-write-the-perfect-logline-and-why-its-as-important-as-your
-screenplay-31710.

19 "Top Box Office Logline Examples," *Film Daily,* January 6, 2022, https://www
.filmdaily.tv/logline/top-box-office-logline-examples.

20 *Rear Window.*

21 Jason Hellerman, "How to Use the Black List to Break Into Screenwriting,"
No Film School, November 3, 2020, https://nofilmschool.com/how-to-use-the
-black-list.

22 "The Real Value of Screenwriting Contests," *Filmmarket Hub*, February
5, 2020, https://medium.com/filmarket-hub-academy/the-real-value-of
-screenwriting-contests-625fe6f66b2c.

23 Bennett Voyles, "Amazon's Impact on Publishing Transforms the Book
Industry," *TechTarget,* January 13, 2021, https://searchaws.techtarget.com/
feature/Amazons-impact-on-publishing-transforms-the-book-industry.

24 Diego Perez, "About," yungpueblo.com, November 1, 2021, https://yungpueblo
.com/about.

25 Ros Barber, "For Me, Traditional Publishing Means Poverty. But Self Publish?
No Way." *The Guardian,* May 18, 2022, https://www.theguardian.com/books/
booksblog/2016/mar/21/for-me-traditional-publishing-means-poverty-but-self
-publish-no-way.

26 Tiffany Hawk, "Should You Self-Publish Your Book? 2 Strong Opinions,"
tiffanyhawk.com, August 7, 2021, https://www.tiffanyhawk.com/blog/faq
-should-i-self-publish-2.

27 Lenny Rachitsky, quoted in "So You Want to Launch a Newsletter: Tips from
Substack," by Patrice Peck, et al., *Andreesen Horowitz,* September 9, 2017,
https://a16z.com/2020/09/17/substack-writers.

28 Thomas Umstattd, Jr., "What Indie Authors Need to Know about Kindle
    Unlimited with Lacy Williams," authormedia.com, March 2, 20220, https://
    www.authormedia.com/kindle-unlimited-indie-authors.

29 Harold Underdown, "Self Publish or Not: Advice from a Traditional
    Publisher," underdown.org, January 29, 2022, https://www.underdown.org/self
    -publish.htm.

30 David Carnoy, "Self-Publishing a Book: 25 Things You Need to Know,"
    CNET, June 13, 2012, https://www.cnet.com/tech/services-and-software/self
    -publishing-a-book-25-things-you-need-to-know.

31 Ros Barber, "For Me, Traditional Publishing Means Poverty. But Self Publish?
    No Way."

32 Jack Conte, quoted in "Patreon CEO Jack Conte on Why Creators Can't
    Depend on Platforms," by Nilay Patel, *The Verge*, June 22, 2021, https://www
    .theverge.com/22543655/patreon-ceo-decoder-interview-jack-conte.

33 "The 2019 National Book Awards Finalists Announced," National Book
    Foundation, October 2019, https://www.nationalbook.org/the-2019-national
    -book-awards-finalists-announced.

34 Kristi Belcamino quoted in "Successful Queries: Agent Stacey Glick and
    'Blessed are Those Who Mourn' by Chuck Sambuchino," *Writer's Digest*,
    October 2, 2015, https://www.writersdigest.com/whats-new/successful-queries
    -agent-stacey-glick-and-blessed-are-those-who-mourn.

35 Alex Christian, personal interview, November 26, 2021.

36 Georgia Perry, personal interview, November 23, 2021.

37 Ibid.

38 Kevin Sampsell, personal interview, July 13, 2021.

39 Kristin Wong, "How to Finally Write Your Nonfiction Book," *New York
    Times*, December 10, 2018, https://www.nytimes.com/2018/12/10/smarter
    -living/how-to-finally-write-your-nonfiction-book.html.

40 Erika Goldman, personal interview, July 13, 2021.

41 "FAQ+CONTACT," Microcosm Publishing, January 8, 2022, https://
    microcosmpublishing.com/faq#submit-manuscripts.

Chapter 8

1 Donald Hall, "Poetry and Ambition," *Kenyon Review* 5, no. 4 (1983): 305.

2 See www.awpwriter.org/guide/overview.

3 James Baldwin, quoted in "The Art of Fiction No. 78," by Jordan Elgrably, *The
   Paris Review,* Spring, 1984, January 29, 2022, https://www.theparisreview.org/
   interviews/2994/the-art-of-fiction-no-78-james-baldwin.

4 When I was at Ohio University, the rumor was that James Franco had applied
   to the program but had noted in his application that he intended to self-fund

his education, and wouldn't need financial aid consideration. He ended up attending several different programs simultaneously (all self-funded, I presume).

5	Kendall Dunkelberg, "Thoughts on the MFA Writing Sample: What Are We Looking For?" kendalldunkelberg.com, February 19, 2015, https://kendalldunkelberg.com/2015/02/19/thoughts-on-the-mfa-writing-sample-what-are-we-looking-for.

6	Cady Vishniac, "How I Wrote My Statement of Purpose," *The Workshop*, October 28, 2015, https://readtheworkshop.com/2015/10/28/how-i-wrote-my-statement-of-purpose.

7	Tom Provost, personal interview, April 22, 2020.

8	Kisha Lewellyn Schlegel, personal interview, February 27, 2020.

9	Alexander Chee, *How to Write an Autobiographical Novel* (Boston: Mariner Books, 2018), 118.

10	Huan Hsu, personal interview, July 30, 2021.

Chapter 9

1	Charles Everit Poverman, "Buzz Poverman: Some Thoughts on the Program," University of Arizona, June 28, 2010, The Internet Archive, January 29, 2022, https://web.archive.org/web/20100628082452/http://english.arizona.edu/index_site.php?id=107&preview=1.

2	Russell Celyn Jones, "Teaching Creative Writing," *The Richmond Review*, January 29, 2022. https://www.richmondreview.co.uk/jones.

3	Alison Flood, "Creative writing professor Hanif Kureishi says such courses are 'a waste of time,'" *The Guardian*, March 4, 2014, https://www.theguardian.com/books/2014/mar/04/creative-writing-courses-waste-of-time-hanif-kureishi.

4	Ryan Boudinot, "Things I Can Say about MFA Writing Programs Now That I No Longer Teach at One," *The Stranger*, February 27, 2015, https://www.thestranger.com/books/features/2015/02/27/21792750/things-i-can-say-about-mfa-writing-programs-now-that-i-no-longer-teach-in-one.

5	Anelise Chen, "On Blowing My Load: Thoughts from Inside the Mfa Ponzi Scheme," *The Rumpus*, October 1, 2010, https://therumpus.net/2010/10/on-blowing-my-load-thoughts-from-inside-the-mfa-ponzi-scheme.

6	Mila Myles, personal interview, September 7, 2021.

7	Nick Gray, personal interview, September 9, 2021.

8	Khara House, personal interview, October 11, 2021.

9	Fareed Zakaria, *In Defense of Liberal Education* (New York: W.W. Norton & Company, 2016), 105.

10	Ibid., 78–9.

11	Liz Lierman, et al., "Internships: Career Outcomes for the Liberal Arts," National Association of Colleges and Employers, May 1, 2017, https://www

.naceweb.org/job-market/internships/internships-career-outcomes-for-the
-liberal-arts.

12   Gina Shereda and Joseph Stanhope Cialdella, "Making the Case for an
     Internship," *Inside Higher Ed,* April 26, 2021, https://www.insidehighered
     .com/advice/2021/04/26/how-talk-your-adviser-about-benefits-internship-your
     -scholarship-and-career.

13   Anu Taranath, *Beyond Guilt Trips* (Toronto: Between the Lines Press, 2020),
     197.

14   John Warner, "To Potential MFA Students: There Are No Academic Jobs,"
     Inside Higher Ed, September 14, 2014, https://www.insidehighered.com/blogs/
     just-visiting/potential-mfa-students-there-are-no-academic-jobs.

15   Karen Kelsky, *The Professor Is In: The Essential Guide To Turning Your Ph.D.
     Into a Job* (New York: Crown Publishing Group, 2015), 96.

16   Phong Nguyen, personal interview, September 4, 2021.

17   Natasha Sajé, "How to Prepare Yourself for the Academic Job Market,"
     AWP, September 2010, https://www.awpwriter.org/magazine_media/
     writers_notebook_view/149/how_to_prepare_yourself_for_the_academic_
     job_market.

18   Victoria Reyes, "Do's and Don'ts for Writing a Cover Letter for the Academic
     Job Market," *Inside Higher Ed*, January 22, 2020, https://www.insidehighered
     .com/advice/2020/01/22/dos-and-donts-writing-cover-letter-academic-job
     -market-opinion.

19   Sajé, "How to Prepare Yourself for the Academic Job Market."

20   Kelsky, *The Professor Is In*, 166.

21   Ibid., 166.

22   Tanya Golash-Boza, "How to Write an Effective Diversity Statement," *Inside
     Higher Ed*, June 10, 2016, https://www.insidehighered.com/advice/2016/06/10/
     how-write-effective-diversity-statement-essay.

23   Dora Malech, "Show Your Joy: Getting Ready and Preparing for an Academic
     Interview," *AWP*, August 2016, https://www.awpwriter.org/magazine_media
     /writers_notebook_view/76/show_your_joy_getting_and_preparing_for_an
     _academic_interview.

Chapter 10

1   Robert hass, quoted in *The Writer's Journal: 40 Contemporary Writers and
     Their Journals*, edited by Sheila Bender (New York: Delta, 1997), 54.

2   Anne Lamott, *Bird by Bird: Some Instructions on Writing and Life* (New York:
    Anchor, 1994), XXVI.

3   Ted Thompson, "Ask a Debut Novelist," *Little Brown*, January 29, 2022,
    https://littlebrown.tumblr.com/post/88988911412/ask-a-debut-novelist
    -question-5-in-which.

4 Ibid.

5 Naomi Shihab Nye, "Re: The Writer's Journal," in *The Writer's Journal*, 238.

6 Diana Abu-Jaber, "The Tenor of Memories," in *The Writer's Journal*, 5.

7 Maurice Manning, personal interview, January 20, 2020.

8 Janet Fitch, personal interview, February 14, 2020.

9 Soraya Duncan, personal interview, October 11, 2021.

10 Thomas Mullen, "The Road Less Traveled: Making It without an MFA," *Poets & Writers Magazine*, August 16, 2017, https://www.pw.org/content/the_road_less_traveled_making_it_without_an_mfa.

11 Amy Berkowitz, personal interview, September 4, 2021.

12 Chris Maier, personal interview, August 7, 2021.

13 Annie Dillard, *The Writing Life* (New York: HarperCollins, 2009), 32.

INDEX